STEPPING STONES
INTO
THE UNKNOWN

VERONIKA STRONG

To Edward
with all my best
wishes

Veronika.

Cyprus, September 1997

Veronika Strong   Stepping Stones Into The Uknown
Published by DFH Publications 1997

DFH Publications
Shinehill Lane
South Littleton
Evesham
Worcs   WR11 5TR
Tel: 01386 833 899
Fax: 01386 833 848
E.Mail: xia07@dial.pipex.com

Illustrations by Honor Stephenson

Cover Page Design by Veronika Strong & Jeanette Wakeman

Printed & Bound by Ebenezer Baylis & Son Ltd, Worcester.

STEPPING STONES INTO THE UNKNOWN

I dedicate this book to my three sons - Frank, Rupert and Ronan. Who have in one way or another suffered due to my ignorance.

This is to say a big thank you to a very special discussion group and all it's influences, during a very memorable month of February 1997, and to all our long suffering friends who have helped knowingly or unknowingly with their support.

In times gone past life's experiences were passed on from the older generation to the younger ones by word of mouth.

The local poacher turned up one day and said, "It is about time that the younger ones learnt how to fish". Not many people had such an opportunity to have a river outside their front door, as we had. "They must know how to treat the river and the fish". Off they went and learnt something we could never have taught them, as we had no experience with the river. The poacher's name was Fox. He always maintained an old fox had to teach the young foxes. They learnt a lot, not that the boys - now grown men - are into poaching, they've never forgotten about fishing and the river.

Life's experiences were passed on without any prejudice.

Being a grandmother, it's about time for me to pass on my life's experiences.

We've all had to learn to walk and find the stepping stones in life - I am sure the same will happen to you.

Good luck!

CHAPTER 1

My upbringing was a very strict one. My father was of a dictatorial nature, and he would not allow me time to day dream. There was only time for practicalities as we all had to survive during and after the second World War in Germany. There was no time for dreaming nor any fairy tales - the only book I had was 'Grimm's Fairy Tales', which were rather cruel stories for a small child in wartime Germany. I certainly was never interested, nor encouraged, in the supernatural, haunted houses or ghost stories.

My father could divine for water and knew about underground water under certain houses. It was my grandfather - a successful builder in a small provincial town in - who divined for water. In the past, German houses would not be built on a site where there was underground water.

My husband Christopher studied Natural Sciences at Cambridge and has always had a scientific approach to all agricultural trial work, which was instilled into him with post graduate studies at Cambridge, The University of the West Indies and in the field. He has also done research work both in Africa and South East Asia. To his trained mind, only results that are proven can give you an answer to what is going on.

He has an imaginative mind and a vivid imagination - unlike me. Neither of us are into religious practices, fringe religions nor believers of any other kind. My answer to any of the unexplained or supernatural was, "I only believe it when I experience it". Famous last words.

Our very first holiday together was shortly after we met. Friends of Christopher had asked us to visit them in Ireland, where they had been living for a few months. In the mid sixties Southern Ireland was very rural with few tourists and even fewer cars. The air was clean, the food fresh and uncontaminated. Allergies were far from my mind and I did not know very much about them, except that I was allergic to cats for which I had been medically tested.

Before the Irish holiday I had bought some new eye make-up. Eye make-up was fairly new on the market in the mid sixties. There was this new feeling of moving away from the preconceptions of the older generation. We were young and free and felt liberated, so why not wear what was an exciting new fashion in clothes as well as make-up. When my eyes swelled up and I could not breathe, I put it down to the wretched cats in the friend's house.

This happened to me quite a few times. Many people in England had cats and everywhere I went there were cats. It took me a long time to realise that the swollen eyelids did not only come from the cats but from the make-up itself.

Some years later we lived in the most idyllic old mill cottage by a lively river and we were much admired for it. We had not been there long before our elder boy began to feel unwell. Nothing too serious, just one cold after another, and every bug going he brought home from school. He was just over six years old. Well, maybe it was the change of climate. It was, after all, his first cold winter, and perhaps missing his friends from Singapore or his father who was away during the week, had something to do with it. He was given the usual drugs to cope with sore throats and colds and a bout of tonsillitis was treated with antibiotics. Still he did not improve. We again put it down to the change of climate; after all, it takes some time to get used to the cold winters.

The younger son, however, escaped it all.

At the same time my children went through a stage of being uncontrollable when travelling in a car. Every weekend we had to collect Christopher from the airport, and had to drive a two hour journey, there and back. Having got to the destination they were given a drink, usually a soft fizzy one. On the way back all hell broke loose. No matter what I did or said, their behaviour was aggressive and beyond reasoning.

One day, I happened to hear a radio programme on hyperactive children and allergies. It took me a little while to realise that it was the soft drink which sent our children off the rails. This was easy to check out. Next weekend when we got to our destination they were given a non fizzy drink. I could hardly believe that their behaviour on the way back was the same as on the way there - sitting in the back of the car chatting to each other. Well, there was a message somewhere!

They soon realised what fizzy drinks in particular did to them. So when they wanted to show off in school or at parties, they would drink fizzy drinks and they were away!

CHAPTER 2

My health has never been the best since my mid twenties and for over twenty years I suffered from severe migraines. They seem to run in my mother's family and I was told to put up with it. In the early days I took any handy drug available, with or without prescription, only to find, nothing helped but to suffer the side effects from the prescribed drugs which were usually as bad as the migraines, and did not help the pain. It was only when the migraines got worse with age (and not better as my mother had predicted) and more frequent, that I started to seek advice again. Hormones, new drugs, preventative drugs - nothing helped. It was only when I was offered Beta Blockers that I stopped seeking advice.

In fact the only time I was really well was as a late teenager in Germany.

Migraines, not being able to sleep and digestive problems seemed to be part of my life. My explanation was the different climate in Ireland, high altitude in Africa and high humidity in Singapore, and that migraines and bad stomach's ran in the family. I felt that I was the one who had inherited the weakest points of both parents. There was nothing I could do about my ill health, and I had no explanation for the non sleeping.

One day, when I was looking more tired than usual, a very good friend of ours told me very excitedly about her new discovery. Like me, she was a very poor sleeper, but she had found a local farmer who was a water diviner[1] and he had discovered that she was sleeping in the wrong place. She and her husband lived in a large rambling house and her bed was in the worst position in this big house.

According to the water diviner, there was a stream of black water running deep down right across the corner of the house where she had her bed. She was advised to move the bed across the room to another wall, which she did. Much to everyone's surprise she immediately began to sleep much better. Despite being more than sceptical, I said to my friend, that I would give her water diviner a try. Instead of phoning, I went to see the farmer for myself.

I met Mrs. Hill outside her back door, a very normal down to earth woman who could not be more welcoming. Her husband came across the yard, and again to my mind, a very normal hardworking farmer. He agreed to come and check our house after I told him my story.

A day or so later he arrived with his rods, walked slowly from one end of the house to the next, seemingly in another world, crossing over the same

---

[1] *DIVINE: (Not in the religious sense) - to search by intuition or to use instinctive insight.*

14

area again and again, with his rods moving in his hands, apparently of their own accord.

Yes, there was a lot of water trapped somewhere under the house deep, deep down; after all, we did live in a mill house. The river flowed into a bend a hundred yards up stream from the house. It was only natural that the water down under the river bed would flow in a straight line. Obviously there were crevices through which the water passed under the house. Strangely the driest end of the house was the one closest to the river. This all made sense to me, as everybody loved sitting in our kitchen which was on the dry side, and in the same place upstairs, where again our friends, including ourselves, loved to sit in the bay window overlooking the river. In latter years that was the only place where I could sleep. Yet the place where the elder boy was sleeping was at the other end of the house away from the river and was certainly not very welcoming; in fact, it was rather creepy even to me. There was obviously an answer to our problems. We moved beds and carpets in all directions; it was an instant success - very much to my surprise!

I began to understand, why at about the same time, a wealthy German acquaintance of ours, who had come to Ireland with the intention of buying a large house used a dowser.[1] The dream of his life was to have a

---

[1] *DOWSE: to search for the unseen, to ask for an answer to the unknown. Examples: Dowsing for water using a forked hazel branch as a divining rod. Dowsing for minerals using angle rods with a reference material. Dowsing for allergies using a pendulum.*

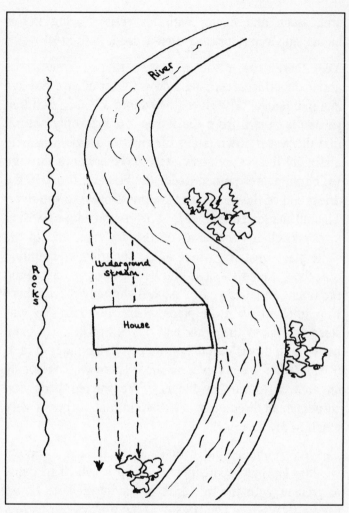

house with an avenue leading to it, and being
surrounded by a few acres of land. When he found it,
he was very taken with the place and wanted to own it
immediately. But despite his impatience, he only
bought it when a German dowser, whom he had
brought to Ireland specially, had given him the O.K

that the place was safe to live in.However, by the time I was forty I had resigned myself to migraines. I had an attack every two to three weeks, and each time this meant three days of being not able to do anything but go to bed in a darkened room - which I hated!

My head split as if into two halves, one side with this incredible sharp pain, the other numb and then as if somebody was trying to tie an iron band tighter and tighter around my head. The daylight - in fact any light - hurt my eyes. To top it all, I would be sick several times during an attack, making my head even worse.

I had heard of a man with the 'gift' who lived very close by, who helped babies and children and adults in the neighbourhood. But somehow it had not occurred to me to seek his advice. It was only when friends urged me to go and see Mr. Thackaberry that I conceded and in desperation made an appointment. He was, like Mr. Hill, a water diviner, but he specialised in divining for allergies and in particular for the 'younger ones', as they said.

I went to see Mr. Thackaberry. He and his wife were retired farmers and lived in a very neat and pleasant looking bungalow. There was certainly no myth about what Mr. Thackaberry was doing. In his comfortable kitchen protected by his wife, the telephone calls came from all over Ireland and abroad asking for help and appointments.

At this stage I wondered why I had not seen Mr. Thackaberry any earlier in my life!

I had never seen anybody using a pendulum[1]. It was rather fascinating. He just held his pendulum over each item on a long food list, to which the pendulum would swing in different directions for things I seemed to be allergic to.

It was only when I got home that I realised my eating habits had to change radically if I wanted to stick to what Mr. Thackaberry had advised me to do. "Cut out all the "No's" for a while and you should be better." Easier said than done, as most of my favourite foods were on the "No" list. In the past I had tried to cut out some of the well known causes of migraine, e.g chocolate, cheese, red wine, coffee. Not altogether, but one at a time to find the one causing my migraine, if indeed it was an allergy to food. But there was no improvement.

I had no choice but to start the next day. I decided it was too time consuming to cut out the offending ingredients one by one. With my list it would take me years! As the next migraine was due soon, I could only do one thing - cut out the lot! This certainly created problems as I was not allowed to eat any flour of any kind. What do I do for bread, biscuits, cake??? No chocolate, red wine, coffee and cheese, nor any other dairy products!

There were more, but those were the main ones in my case. My new food regime was certainly a challenge. I

---

[1] *PENDULUM - Suspended weight swinging to & fro.*

hate reading labels - it's time consuming and awkward when you can't see the small print.

But, from now on, I had to read all the labels on each item bought, as even stock cubes and mustard, bottled sauces and curry powders contain starch. (Starch of course is usually flour). It was tedious but I persevered and, after three weeks the withdrawal symptoms stopped. I waited for my next migraine. It was bound to come at that time of the month - nothing happened! I waited five weeks, still in anticipation, six weeks, two months, three months - no migraine. I felt altogether so much better.

All other symptoms of a having blown-up stomach, and stomach acidity had all vanished as well! In fact, all of a sudden I felt so much better. I had lost excessive weight and was a different person. To this day (which is ten years later) I am extremely well, and migraines and all other complaints have faded into the past.

Mr. Thackaberry had long lists of successfully curing ill people, in one case, merely by just changing their brand of orange juice. How did the divining[1] rods and the pendulum work? I had spoken to people who could not stick to their regime of cutting out their offending foods and their complaint had not gone away! I was now in a dilemma. Moving beds and combating

---

[1] *DIVINING ROD - Either a forked hazel stick, or L-shaped metal rods held in a dowser's hands to show the presence of underground water.*

allergies in a non scientific way was not really how I wanted to look at the problem. Even though it had worked for me.

Was it witchcraft?

Well, neither Christopher nor I had any inclination to believe in anything like that. There must be an explanation somewhere, but for the moment we had to be content that dowsing really did work. We started to read about it but the literature gave no real explanation either.

In a small community such as Ireland, news spread quickly and we heard this fascinating story. A Biochemist had come to see one of the dowsers, bringing with him details of several alternative treatments for his wife. She was seriously ill and had not long to live, unless the right treatment was found quickly.

But, the trials which had been set up to find it would take too long. Our friend was asked to dowse the different treatments for this man's wife. Which he did.

The man went back, started the treatment indicated by the pendulum and his wife responded immediately. Shortly afterwards the results of the medical tests confirmed the result indicated by the pendulum.

Our own dowsing started very much later. Some of my allergies had been sorted out, but there were so many foods which were not on my list and others where the labels did not specify exactly what was in them. I had made a few mistakes, and had been 'punished' with a number of headaches, (not migraines) obviously by eating the wrong food.

We started to search for more books on the subject. There are a number of books with case histories and there was enough evidence to persuade us to try to see for ourselves if dowsing would work for us. We started off with a beginner's book of dowsing, had various 'trial runs' with a lot of fun - it worked!! We got terribly excited when the pendulum held over glasses of water gave us the right answers. It says in the books, that in fact everybody can dowse!

It opened a whole new world for us.

I then started dowsing when I went shopping. I would not read the labels anymore but just dowsed over the products. Providing I could relax my mind, it worked. I made a few mistakes. The wishful thinking part is very strong and then dowsing won't work. Make a mistake - get a headache! So in the end I learnt that I just had to give in, let the right hand side of my mind take over and trust my pendulum.

Our dowsing for our own purposes became more and more extensive - from planting which plants, and knowing which spacing to use, to building an entire house - with very surprising results.

Our dowsing has brought us so much happiness and many challenges that we feel we must pass on our experiences which have saved our lives and restored our health. We are both looking and feeling much younger than we did ten years ago. Seeing the amazement on people's faces when Christopher says "I'm sixty this year" must be some proof of it!

We came to the conclusion, that if your body does not have to waste its energy by fighting all the wrong ingredients in its food, and if you are sleeping in a safe place, you feel very happy and positive. No pills or drugs can give you such a boost of well-being.

The fizzy drink story is now some years back, and one can only wonder what present day foods with all their additional chemicals do to us; and worse what they do to our children. If mothers would dowse over their babies' food what confidence it would give them to know they are getting what is right for them. This of course would eliminate a lot of uncertainty. Babies and children would grow up much healthier, so many problems would be avoided, as their immune systems would be intact. Their bodies would not have to fight the ingredients in our food that the human system is not used to. On the other hand, we would know for certain that some additives and chemicals will not do us any harm. I can only quote from my own experience. If I dowse over organic potatoes for instance it says "No" to me - no offence is intended to any organic farmer - it's just me! Whatever the reason I don't know, but I do accept the fact I can't eat organic potatoes. Yet at this stage I can drink a certain brand of coffee and eat lots of spicy food.

More often than not in the past when I went shopping I thought to myself, oh well, I'll pick this one up quickly, I am after all in a hurry and I am sure it will be all right. I have been sorry about this attitude. In the long run it does not pay off. The food picked up in a hurry contains something I can't eat or worse, if I did eat it I would get a headache. So convenience yes, but it all has to be checked out.

You have to be realistic and practical about modern day living but you also have to sit back and think about the implications, particularly for your children. It takes so little time to dowse over our food to make sure it contains no ingredients that are poisonous and allergic to their and our systems. I cannot stress enough that this is different for each one of us.

Why do so many people, even children, suffer from [1]M.E.?

There is no definition of the disease nor a test to prove it. Is it not self evident, that if a body is to cope with many new ingredients in its digestive system, unknown in its history, that it will have to spend valuable energy and time absorbing and dealing with all these new things?

Just imagine spending all your energy fighting off intruders (e.g. ingredients in our food) which you don't know how to cope with, and after that being put to bed in possibly an unsafe place, then being hammered by geopathic stress[2]. What would your

---

[1] *M.E. - Chronic Fatigue Syndrome*

[2] *GEOPATHIC STRESS - Disturbance caused by subterranean water and Earth energy affecting our health - this is explained in detail later on.*

immune system say? "To hell with this, can't cope, I switch off and break down." Especially if you are already weakened by say, a bout of 'flu, your body simply cannot recover it's strength and this then can become M.E.

CHAPTER 3

I have seen people with different complaints. I will go through their diet and where they sleep. The comment I get beforehand is that they presume that they are doing something wrong. "Oh, I can't eat chocolate anymore", or "I will have to give up smoking"!

This is the logical answer. But dowsing works from the right hand side of the brain - in other words our intuitive[1] or instinctive[2] side, and there is no logic to it. I have often found, that people can eat chocolate and can smoke a few cigarettes a day without too much harm, and the offending food turns out to be a totally unexpected one. So why don't we make our lives and that of our children simpler?

Babies and young children will know instinctively what is good for them. They reject certain foods either by being sick, or suffering from colic and tummy pains. Babies don't usually cry for no reason.

Even breastfed babies can experience colic and tummy pain. This is usually because the baby does not like something which the mother has eaten. I am sure

---

[1] *INTUITION: an inner conviction, insight or knowing.*

[2] *INSTINCT: biological programming and reaction, without seeming to use conscious thought.*

every breast feeding mother will know that too much alcohol will be passed on to the baby through her own milk. So what about the cabbage and the baked beans? Dowse over your own food and you will know what not to eat next time!

The first problem arises when you are not breast feeding - which milk formula to feed your baby on? The choices are numerous but which one is the right one for your baby? Well, you don't know. You ask friends, the nurse who comes to see you, your mother maybe, but nobody really knows which is the right formula for your baby. Trial and error. Upset tummies, crying and sleepless nights. What to do? Nobody has enough time to spend hours examining every aspect of your baby's life unless it becomes very ill, when it will be treated with some pills or drops - which could have been avoided! By dowsing, of course, we will know immediately which milk formula would suit your baby best - that is if you are not breastfeeding. And then all is well, crying is at a minimum, you can enjoy longer nights and everybody should be happy.

There is also the question of which washing powder, soap and shampoo is good not only for one's baby, but for older children and yourself. Rows upon rows are on offer in the shops. The other day I spent some time dowsing over baby shampoos and I was horrified with the result. I wondered why, and spent more time reading the labels. The ingredients all have very complicated names now, and nobody, apart from the people who manufacture these, will know what they mean. So we think, "Oh, well it says on telly that they are good for you, so they must be right". They are not!

If you don't understand the ingredients, you have no idea what they do to you and your children's skin and health. If you dowse over them with your baby in mind, you will find the right one. The same goes for soap and, in particular, washing powder. Try to dowse over the fabric softeners. The advertisements always use babies or small children to appeal to your subconscious, to persuade you to do the best for them by buying that particular product. By the time you notice any skin problems, it is too late, but we could have avoided all this, by just buying the right product in the first place!

Later on, when your baby is starting to eat solid food, there are all sorts of appetising jars for them (and us)

to taste. But, how do you know that your baby is not allergic to apricots or any other ingredient in that particular brand of baby food?

It's so easy to check!

Our youngest son, to this day cannot eat eggs. When he was a baby he would let me know all right - out it all came again. I soon learnt - leave it out in future. With the eldest it was fish. I spent a lot of time cleaning up the mess, but had I been able to dowse I would have known better beforehand. By dowsing it is possible to feed your child with a diet that is right for it and chances are that it will thrive. If you don't know that you are feeding it the wrong food, your baby will be upset and it will cry as this is the only way it can tell you something is wrong.

The same also applies to choosing nappies. Are all nappy's whichever brand, good for your baby's skin? The advertisements say so, but how do you know? If you don't check, it might be painful for your baby and you to find out!!

In no way would any mother want to feed her baby something which would cause an upset or cannot be digested or use irritants on the delicate skin. Dowsing enables mothers to understand their babies much better.

A lot has been written about mattresses in babies' cots and cot death. You can check yourself whether the mattress and it's innards are causing your baby any breathing difficulty. Or is there any other reason?

I am always horrified to see small children and babies 'locked up' under plastic covers in their push chairs. Is there enough air in the 'capsule', and when it's hot does this plastic release any poisonous substances. You don't know unless you check.

Very often I have observed how babies and small toddlers are put into their push chairs and then taken for a walk amongst heavy traffic, amongst hurrying people. The proud grandparents or harassed mothers push these push chairs in front of them, often with anxious little faces looking out. They can't see this of course, as the child faces the other way. Has it ever occurred to the families, that a small child might be frightened and confused by trucks, buses, cars, people and noise? Small babies and children need to be in contact with a reference person - mother, grandmother, fostermother, au pair or whoever. Just put yourself into your baby's situation. It only knows Mum and it's own surroundings, and suddenly it is faced with all these strange moving things. Why can't we just turn the seat of the push chair towards us, so at least the baby has something it recognises in this strange world. Follow your instinct and you will know! In other words dowse which way your baby should be facing.

My six year old nephew came to stay with us during holiday time. He was a very fussy eater and only wanted to have honey on his bread, to which his parents objected. We checked him out and found that he was extremely allergic to salt. We changed his diet. He soon began to love his food. When he went back home to his parents, they did not believe what he was telling them. His father continued to insist that he eat crisps and hearty meals with lots of German cold meats which, of course, contain salt.

That boy is now twelve years old, small and slight in stature although his parents are tall and well built. He looks extremely pale and is still pushed into eating things he does not want. A slow fussy eater!

If you ever have a chance to watch wild birds feed, it will give you a good insight. Do wild birds and animals pick up strange food items which would not be good for them? No, they don't. We were watching a cock pheasant with his two hens working their way across a field feeding. Christopher said to me, "Aren't they fussy birds?" Well, no, they are not, they only pick up food which they know they can eat. Do we do the same?

When I was a small child I hated fish, yet my mother forced me to eat it. Result - I was sick all over the kitchen, for which I then was punished.

There is no question about it, I am allergic to fish!

Children instinctively know what is good for them - apart from the sweets and junk offered to them on TV and in the supermarkets, which they then of course ask for. How often have I watched small children wanting apples or bananas or other fruit in a supermarket and mother saying no. But, from what was in her trolley, it was not the money she was worried about. Does the mother know why the children were refused something good for them? Yet she allowed them sweets at the exit.

All young children have the same instinct - unless they are too influenced by TV ads - but a dowsing mother could tell!

Drinking and eating things you are allergic to will become an addiction, which you find very difficult to stop under normal circumstances. I used to drink seven to ten cups of instant coffee a day, and I craved for more. The number of cups were on the increase, the same for bread, biscuits and cakes. When I had a migraine attack I would then eat dry toast hoping to get rid of the sickness feeling. Invariably, it made my migraine worse. I know now that I can't eat bread and drink instant coffee as I am allergic to them. It was a vicious circle - craving and allergy.

CHAPTER 4

In Germany, if the swallows nest under the roof of your house, it is thought to bring you luck. In many other countries, including Britain, the old wives' tale was that the stork brings all the babies. Why the stork? Well, there is a perfectly reasonable explanation. Storks - when there were still plenty of them - would nest on top of certain houses and not on others. It seemed that the houses with stork nests would have many more and healthier children than the others. The truth is that the storks would only nest on top of safe houses, which in our terms today means houses free of geopathic stress, in other words, those built with no water or harmful earthrays under them.

We have a friend who was desperate to get pregnant as she was happily married and all the circumstances were right for her to have a family. She was already in her mid thirties and was becoming slightly concerned that she had not conceived. She was living in a house in Ireland which unknown to her had a history of no young families ever living there. The elderly people in the area used to say that there was no chance of getting pregnant in that house. What a daunting prospect! Eventually, we dowsed all over the house, and it certainly was not a happy one. She only became pregnant when they went on a long beach holiday, after which they sold the house.

If you are desperate for a family and have not conceived, get a local dowser to check out your house before you do anything else! If your house is on a geopathically stressed site, conception will be much more difficult, if not impossible.

Our concern with the well-being of our children should really start with conception.

From the moment of conception the future child's health can be influenced simply by dowsing over the mothers food and environment. During early pregnancy there is competition between the foetus and the mother, hence the morning sickness and cravings, but once everything settles down, all should become harmonious. Then baby will start to dictate to the mother's body by demanding more blood, hence the possibility of higher blood pressure, but under normal circumstances, this only persists until the baby is born. Particularly during pregnancy dowse over your food to avoid unnecessary stress on your system.

There is a strong correlation between cot deaths and geopathic stress. So, before you get your baby's room fitted out, it is necessary to check this. By the time you have completed this book, this will not be a problem for you.

We spent a number of years in Africa and women there, certainly do not have the medical care women have here. Nor do they, to my mind have the same problems of childbirth.

I have seen women there crouching in the fields having their babies with much less discomfort than women here with all the medical attention.

Nowadays, an epidural seems to be nearly a normal procedure. Unborn babies are put onto monitors, mothers are also on drips and more monitors. The clips - with it's jump leads - are fastened onto your unborn baby's head and must be painful, as it leaves a mark and can even penetrate the skin. In some cases the scars can be seen for years. It is amazing what we allow other people to do to us and our babies!

When I had my children, epidurals for childbirth were very new on the market and there were no baby monitors. I did not want to run the risk of having an injection into my spine! I am not arguing that childbirth isn't painful. Yes, it is, but what all these women are missing, is something they will not experience with an epidural. The pain is soon gone, but that feeling of elation is never forgotten.

When the baby's head is through, not only is the worst pain over but there is an immense physical pleasure when the rest of the baby is being born. I would not have liked to miss this for anything. The same feeling was confirmed to me by friends who did not have epidurals either.

Women are still made to lie down in some cases, although I am sure it is much improved now, but lying down, is the worst position for a woman to give birth. It is completely unnatural and possibly only for the convenience of the people who are delivering the baby.

It's time for women to take control of their own lives. Once you can dowse, you can decide for yourself which way you are going to have your baby, at what stage of labour you should go into hospital or stay at home (if you want that), which position will be best for you to deliver your baby, and if you should have an epidural or not. Might not a monitor (which after all is an electrical machine) put extra stress on your unborn baby on its difficult passage in to the world?

During your pregnancy, you will have enough time, to dowse all these unknown things for yourself. During the ante-natal sessions available to everybody, you will learn what is going to happen to you. It will give you the chance to decide for yourself what to do. You can find out if your unborn baby is doing well and if not, why not? Please don't get me wrong. If there is the slightest chance, that you need medical attention, you must seek it. But, if everything is going all right for you, why not have it your way, which will be the best for your baby and you? You don't need people shouting at you to push, whilst wired up to all sorts of electrical machines. That will only increase the stress on you both.

Once you know what is happening to you during pregnancy and labour, then you can go ahead with a quiet self-confidence knowing it will work. And yes, enjoy childbirth as an even more special occasion.

Baby arrives and wow - stress instead of quiet joy!

A sheep farmer's greatest concern at lambing is that the new-born lambs get their first milk from the mother very quickly. This first milk contains colostrum, a substance which provides immunity to infection for the first vital months. The same applies to us humans. We often deny our babies this valuable start by not providing them with that important immunity which is contained in our own milk but not in any milk formulas. It has been proven that women who breastfeed their babies are much less likely to develop breast cancer in later years.

When we discussed the main food problems that people have with our Irish dowser friend Mr. Thackaberry, the number one problem was baby food. Parents have great difficulties in finding the correct food that their children could thrive on. In Ireland, there was at that time a lot of pressure on mothers to forget about breast feeding and use the bottle. It was thought to be easier, not only for the hospital but when returning home - anybody could feed the baby. Difficult to understand? There was also social pressure, as bottle feeding was thought to be more modern.

The result was a stream of anxious mothers with babes in arms with colic and breathing problems. Mr. Thackaberry's speciality was finding the right milk formula, and often persuading mothers with toddlers to discontinue cows milk. Change to the right formula and the children would be happier and content. Take away the irritant and the children would be well.

We happened to be in a very smoky pub the other day. To my horror there was a non-smoking mother with her tiny baby sitting in a corner. I wondered did she know what she was doing to her child?

Had she been able to dowse, she would have known what to do. Just dowse over that cigarette and then over the smoke and ask about the smoke and the implications of passive smoking, at such a tender age when lungs are not even fully developed. Dowse and see what answer you get from the pendulum.

I often wish that if I had been able to dowse when our children were babies it would have saved me and them a lot of anguish, and the stress of the unknown could instead, have been happiness and joy.

If you take your sick animal to the Vet, he will always ask: "What have you been feeding it on?" But, will a doctor ask the same question to try to find out the reason why your child is ill?

Doctors are very busy people and are trained to treat symptoms if something has gone wrong with our health. No way has a practitioner time to go through endless lists of food to check if we are allergic to some of it. The costs of such tests would be prohibitive and the procedure is too lengthy.

Although traditional medicine should, in all fairness, find underlying causes of ill health, in the majority of cases, people get sent home with some pills, maybe followed by a test later on, but not many questions will be asked!

By the time you have finished reading this book you will be able to dowse over your baby's, children's and your own food. Make yourself a list of what they are eating in the course of a week - not the amounts but the brand name and check everything out yourself.

CHAPTER 5

Often children and adults do not get better after some prolonged medical treatment and the use of different drugs. In cases like that, obviously further questions should be asked! Is that person sleeping in a safe place, eating the right diet? If you could dowse yourself, it would save a lot of uncertainty and you can check yourself, if you and your children sleep in a safe place. Then you can avoid unnecessary illness and distress.

By dowsing yourself, you can have the proof very quickly. Just cut the offending ingredient out of your diet, move your bed or chair to a safe place - and see. I myself have had no reason to consult a doctor about anything serious for the last ten years. It does not mean that I would reject any treatment or drugs, but I just have not been ill. That to me is proof enough, that my dowsing must be right.

So, why do we get ill or have long-lasting health problems? In the days of hunting and fishing for our food, it was clear that nothing was eaten which was manufactured or treated in any way; no vegetable or corn was grown with pesticides or fungicide treatment, nor were any artificial fertilisers used. Well, that was some time back. With increasing technology, research and healthcare people live longer and the population is on the increase. In order to keep up with this, obviously our methods of producing food had to change. What we haven't catered for is that our bodies need a bit longer to adjust to all these changes. But how do you cope with them in the meantime? Allergic reactions in the form of digestive problems, skin problems, hyperactivity in children, migraines and headaches for no obvious reason, are all very real and painful. Often drugs do not cure the problems and you are then categorised as a hypochondriac, difficult or lazy. Often it only needs a small change in your life and you could be a different person again. But why does it happen in the first place? We all have some weak points in our bodies, inherited or otherwise, and these of course are the first areas to break down. If our immune systems are constantly hammered and cannot regain full strength they won't be efficient and - 'bang' - down we go!

We all know what happens if any part of a car is put through too much wear and tear. It breaks down and stops until we find the cause. Repair it, and it will go again! It is the same with our bodies. The weakest points will give in and we will suffer the symptoms of sickness for which we then have to be treated. Do we look for the cause??

Why wait until your immune system breaks down? It is much easier to encourage your body and that of your children's to strengthen their immune systems and thus to protect their weakpoints.

For any overweight person, it is easy by dowsing to find which ingredients in their diet are causing the problem - simply cut them out - this may be all that is needed without going on numerous diets!

In the Middle Ages people were old when they reached the age of forty-five or fifty. Their bodies were by that time worn out with malnutrition, disease and what we would think of as sheer discomfort. At least in the developed countries, education, better hygiene, healthcare and modern day living have not only doubled our life expectation, but it is expected that people will live even longer.

We will of course expect to live well, and some of us expect to live an active and happy life even longer. Huge funds are being spent into research on how we can prolong our lives, but most people (including the researchers) have forgotten to look at the basics, which will prolong life, without any effort or cost.

We should be willing to listen to our bodies, - when I mentioned this to a friend and told her at the same time that she couldn't eat onions, she answered, that she had always thought this! Why then did she eat the onions! Because she was uncertain and not used to listening to her body. Had she listened to her body or (in other words, her intuition) she would have been saved a lot of discomfort.

I am not somebody who follows a guru, the latest vitamin craze or any other drugs, hoping to improve my lot. I do not meditate nor do any fitness exercises for hours, nor do I follow any stream of new found ideas around the world.

I am not trying to be smart and know it all. There are many things in our lives which we don't understand, nor can they be scientifically proven; such as you contact a friend - "Oh, I was just thinking of you", is the answer. Telepathy. Everybody must have experienced telepathy; think of a person subconsciously and in short you will hear from them. You pick up the phone and find that the person you wanted to ring was trying to phone you at the same time! Or, a friend appears in your mind whom you haven't heard from for some time, and again there will be a contact out of the blue regardless of where they are in the world. These phenomena cannot be explained; nor can the phenomenon of dowsing. Yet, with dowsing we can help ourselves or an experienced dowser can help you with any greater problems which you don't have the confidence to tackle.

But where did all this dowsing come from?

CHAPTER 6

There is little doubt that the Chinese were familiar with earth energies as far back as 4000 years ago. They called geopathic stressed areas dragon lines, and no-one could build their houses on a dragon line. The Feng Shui masters call it 'angry energy'.

Dowsing is an ancient practice originally carried out to find safe sites for people to be buried. The Egyptian pyramids could well have been built with the help of dowsers. The alignment and illustrations from the time of building the pyramids show that dowsing was very well understood. It is further presumed that Cleopatra was surrounded by two dowsers at all times. And it is thought that most ancient people knew about dowsing. Holy places, and later, churches were built on specific sites and a dowser would either have the main say or be consulted, as we know from the Druids. Moses was supposed to have been an excellent dowser.

What went so wrong that we lost all sight of this skill and only a few people have kept dowsing going on the quiet?

There was a time when the city of Alexandria in Egypt was the centre of the trading world. It had the biggest library of knowledge which was burned down by a fanatical mob some thirty years B.C. All knowledge that was valuable was lost. These events were repeated throughout history, by different fanatical groups, even to this day.

Later the church hierarchy was afraid of competition from people whom they could not control, and would not allow knowledge to be passed on unexplained and uncensored. Dowsers and evidence alike were destroyed.

The Knights Templars were guardians of the Temple of Solomon in the Holy Land during the Crusades. They had an incredible knowledge of all aspects of life. They returned to Europe to what is now largely France. They were responsible for a complete revolution in soaring architecture that carried all the aspirations of that age to a breathtaking peak. The cathedrals - given the materials they were using, seem even today to be impossible. They returned with a new found knowledge that was uncanny in it's accuracy and precision from the crusades.

Their seat from where they ruled was the exact middle of a landmass. How did they know the exact centre of the lands that were under their control, without technical equipment for measuring distances.

Their secrets and knowledge died with them when they were all exterminated at the beginning of the 14th Century to a man by jealous rulers. Friday 13th October saw the end of the Templars - and to this day Friday 13th is still regarded as an unlucky day.

What did the Knights Templars know, and how did they gain this knowledge which is lost to us? Did history repeat itself yet again? - A history dowser could tell you!

It is only in recent times that the churches hierarchy have given their blessings to help people to live in houses free of geopathic stress, and it maybe comforting to know that the expression of 'Bishops Rule' is the name for depth measure when finding water.

It is interesting that most of the very old churches were sited on places where earth energy is emanating, and a short time of exposure to this energy is beneficial. These sites were known to pre-date the building of churches, that means of course that ancient people knew more then we give them credit for.

We know, from the position of the ancient stone circles (the wooden ones having disappeared with time) were erected to enable the people to know when the winter nights stopped, days were getting longer and gave cause to celebrate important days in the year.

Dowsing however, has been passed on quietly between the generations - how many women have to this day had the sex of their child determined by a wedding ring swung from a hair?

Inevitably in time much has become lost and it takes a long time to re-discover this lost knowledge.

We are fortunate now with such an open society throughout most of the world that it is possible to communicate and to help each other.

CHAPTER 7

To divine or dowse for water is to this day, an accepted practice. A dowser will find the right place where to find water. So why not help ourselves with the same methods in checking out where we sleep and that we eat the right food?

Although it is difficult for our trained and unintuitive mind to understand how dowsing works, we just have to accept the fact that it does work.

Trials have been done with young children to see if they are able to dowse and, not surprisingly, it worked for most of them at pre-school age. It is only when they started going to school and their brains were trained to read and write (which means using the left hand side of the brain), that this ability started to vanish. By the time the same children were ten years old, only very few could still dowse.

Our own children should have grown up bilingual. They did not. Christopher travelled extensively during the time when our boys were small, and was away for long periods of time. It would have been unfair if I had insisted on them speaking German, they would not have been able to talk to their father. So they spoke only English in a multi-lingual society. I was 'attacked' by Christopher's German boss at the time "Why do your children not speak German?" So with that I went to consult the Headmaster of the German School and it proved that my instinct had been right. He explained that quite a number of his pupils were multi-lingual and none of them could speak one language properly. However, in his opinion, it was important for the children to start a foreign language before the age of nine. The age of eight or nine years seems to be a watershed in children's minds.

I read an article, written by a lady guide looking after small children in a museum, introducing them to paintings. Before the age of nine it does not matter to children if paintings are abstract, contemporary or old masters. They can comprehend the content, and identify with time and colour. But, after that age that intuitive understanding goes and thinking falls into categories or what we would call little boxes??

CHAPTER 8

People have for a long time wondered how birds in the wild know what to eat, when to choose the right mate, when to breed, when and where to fly and how to get there without a map.

In Autumn swallows and other migratory birds congregate on telephone wires and fly as a flock away from us. They haven't got a watch or a calendar, nor does anybody tell them where and when to go. These birds fly South mainly to Africa, some to Spain and other places. Every Spring the same birds will return back to the same nesting places which they left the year before. Even if the old nest is not there anymore, they know which house or tree to go to. These birds are not very big and their brains are tiny compared to ours, but they navigate a complicated route, and know how to avoid bad storms and other natural hazards. They know - what we call instinct - yet nobody questions it!

If we had to do the same journey without any aid or equipment, we would find it virtually impossible.

In the case of hibernating animals like mice and hedgehogs - how do they know when and what to store for winter? They have no books either! In Ireland some elderly people with a 'gift' could tell what the year would be like - particularly winter - by just observing the animal behaviour. If mice, moles and others provide themselves with bigger stores of food than usual, we know it's a sign of a harsh winter to come. But how do these animals know that in autumn they must gather more food? What the animals know, we call instinct. As we know they make few mistakes. Yet when <u>we</u> have an intuition - which is the same thing - we don't want to know!

When the birds migrate these vast distances from the North to the South and back from the South to the North to their birthplace, they rely on their sixth sense or instinct!

Our own recognised senses are seeing, tasting, hearing, smelling and touching. Yet we don't acknowledge our sense of instinct or sixth sense which after all is so often quoted.

The left hand side of our brain is used for logic, mathematics, time and language. The right hand side of our brain is the intuitive side, which is our artistic side, creative, musical and caring. Intuitive means inner tuition, teaching from within or sixth sense. These are largely associated with female characteristics.

Is it then so surprising that women find dowsing easier to understand than men? Men often insist on their logical side of their trained mind, and it is more difficult to give way to the intuitive right hand side. It was when church doctrine was taken over by the male profession that dowsing was condemned and there was no more place for female intuition, which was then seen as a threat.

I will be accused of being sexist and if so, never mind.

I personally find it much easier to get into a dowsing mode than my husband, and I will often be more accurate. He finds it much more difficult to dowse 'at a drop of a hat', and has to clear his mind first, then cannot be disturbed during dowsing.

But on the other hand there are quite a number of scientists, engineers and doctors, who, have discovered for themselves that dowsing works. They use dowsing in their work as well as helping other people.

We all have heard the remark that a person must have a sixth sense or 'having been protected' or was 'protected by an angel', when they escaped unharmed from a potentially serious accident.

All his life Christopher has had the feeling of 'somebody looking after him'. The most memorable event was when, in his student days, he had a car accident in Trinidad. The car hit a pothole in the dark, turned over, slid along on its roof, turned over again, rolled down an embankment and landed on its wheels.

When Christopher woke up, he found himself still sitting behind the steering wheel, by that time a lot of people were around him, and a deep black voice said, "Man, somebody was looking after you!" In those days there were no safety belts. He only had a few scratches on his head and hands. (I am sure the rum had helped with the other pains!)

When my sister was a few days old my mother left her quite safely in her basket on the bathroom floor. Unexpectedly a heavy towel rail dropped out of the wall just above her head miraculously missing her.

How, we did not know! My mother exclaimed "Oh, she must have had a protecting angel!"

We all, I am sure, know a story like that.

With mobile phones, TV and satellite, birds and animals, we accept that unseen information works, so why not our own intuitions, sixth sense, inner voice or dowsing?

However, the use of dowsing for finding water is well accepted as many of us know. That means, if anybody wants to sink a well either on farmland, or in their own garden, or on an industrial site, a well-digging company will be asked to do the job. After that what happens, and how is it done? A well-digging company usually employs a water diviner. Who at first, will start by divining the place in question on a map or drawing, for which he might use a pendulum. The diviner will then in his mind ask the right questions for water, and where to find it. His pendulum will then indicate the area on the map of where to find water. Later the diviner will go on site, re-check the area indicated by his pendulum either a forked hazel stick or L rods made out of metal. As soon as he walks over the place where there is any water, the hazel stick will twitch and point or the rods will cross. It has been proven that water diviners are correct in nearly all cases.

If you were fortunate enough to watch a water diviner, it is absolutely fascinating. He can accurately determine with the swings of his pendulum how deep down the water can be found. He also can tell how much water and at what flow rate it can be pumped out.

In Canada the same dowsing practice is used by people who have to find broken or damaged cables and pipe lines, usually - in a case of emergency. If there is a leak or a broken pipe somewhere in this vast country, dowsers can find it on a map with their pendulum. This takes no time compared to a ground or air search in all weathers. Repair work can then start in the right place immediately. It sounds quite incredible, but it is a fact.

In the United States dowsers are dowsing for healing and to help confirm diagnosis, diets and treatments. They dowse for geopathic stress and earth energies, as well as searching for oil and minerals, prospecting for gold and other metals. They find water, locate missing persons, find fish and game animals, solve mechanical and electrical problems.

In India, dowsers find water for the villages. The same applies to the third world agencies. They also use dowsers to find water all over Africa and S. America.

In Austria, dowsing is much more readily accepted than here in Britain. A site will usually have to be checked for geopathic stress as a pre-condition for planning permission. Doctors, nurses, architects, designers and the ordinary persons use dowsing in their everyday life.

In an extensive scientific research programme it was proven in Austria, Germany and Switzerland that cancer is connected with the incidence of harmful earth rays. When I learnt these facts, I accepted that we can't see, hear or feel these rays, but have to trust our own skill with the pendulum.

There are countries where skilled and experienced dowsers work as holistic healers, herbalists, dieticians and all related areas, together with the hospital staff and the medical profession to save pain, time and money. Yet here in England (and I am sure in other countries as well) the medical profession works on its own. Dowsing may be considered as unacceptable to their status!

However, it must be in the interest of the patient, that dowsing for health should be used in a complementary way with the medical profession and hospitals. On the continent it is not uncommon for hospitals and doctors to use dowsers on a permanent basis, not only to assist diagnosis but also to consider the whole person, and to look at the location where the patient lives and works in order to find out why the illness occurred. To do that the dowser does not have to go to the patients home or workplace! In the hospitals, dowsers help to speed up the healing process, by putting beds and operating tables in geopathically safe areas. Thus, also saving precious funds, reducing waiting times and misery. Dowsing gives the answer almost instantly.

It is common practice, for homeopaths to use dowsing to confirm not only which treatment to use, but also which is the best dosage for each particular patient; and of course as a diagnostic aid.

I have mentioned the importance of sleeping in safe place a number of times now. Let me explain this further.

How often does a friend, a neighbour say "Oh, I don't sleep, I was awake all night" or, "the children kept me awake" and so on. Many children are tired, listless, unable to concentrate, they have no energy, and are aggressive. They find it hard to get on in school, and some suffer from learning difficulties. A lethargic or aggressive child is no fun to live with. But it is no fun for the child either. Crying at night, bed wetting, bad dreams, the list is endless.

Why is it that way? And what can we do?

The middle of the Earth is hot and steamy, which we can see when a volcano erupts. Lava and hot steam are being spat out under enormous pressure. When the hot steam cannot burst through pressure holes, hot springs or volcanoes, it stays underground. There it travels between the layers of rock until it cools down to become water and forms underground streams. These move freely under great pressure, fill any cavity, and hence form the basis of our water sources.

This water is clean, otherwise known as 'white water'. Where a natural gap in the rocks occurs, water flows out. These are usually the springs of a river. But, not all the water comes to the surface. There is a whole array of underground lakes, streams and pools where the water has been caught in the cavities.

This subterranean water creates electro magnetic fields, whose rays rise up to the surface of the earth. It is this electro magnetic energy which is effecting us as geopathic stress.

However, most of our own water comes from some of the wells deep down, being tapped and brought up by pipes. This is the job of a well digging company.

What happens to all the rain water that falls?

Rain water hits the ground and seeps through the soil, sand, gravel, rock and chalk and can end up in underground streams. Sometimes this water can be contaminated, either from pollution in the air being washed down, or organic or chemical deposits on the land. On it's way down water can also go through stone layers containing minerals, which dissolve and will be picked up on the way. We call this polluted water - 'Black water'!

With all the energies coming from the boiling middle of the Earth, there is not only steam and water moving about down there. Imagine a boiling cauldron and all

the ongoing's. Our Earth is the same. We are in fact living on a huge molten magnet. When things get shoved around it produces this enormous energy. When a volcano erupts or an earthquake upsets everything only then do we realise that the middle of the earth is a huge source of energy.

The surface of the earth is just like the skin of boiled milk or a rice pudding. Underneath the skin the rice pudding will produce bubbles from the heat of the cooker. Our Earth is similar. The 'skin' is the cooled down part and represents the surface of the Earth on which we live. In an earthquake or earth tremor, vast plates of rock get moved and shifted, upsetting underground streams, rocks and everything else in a wide area with apparently no consequences for us??

CHAPTER 9

Well, everybody has heard about rays of various kinds, but none of them can be seen or touched. X-rays, cosmic rays, UV, radar, TV, radio and telephone.

The same applies to Earth rays. They can't be seen either.

But, as with everything in life there are good rays and bad rays. If you sleep above the bad rays, they will certainly do your health no good. If you are not able to dowse or are still sceptical, just observe your animals. Dogs will always lie in the good ray places while cats will always seek the bad ray places. I will be accused now of not liking cats - no I don't like cats but this has nothing to do with the matter. This fact has been proven. Horses, dogs, birds like the 'good' places.

There are some other animals and insects which like bad ray places. Ants are one of them. If you find an anthill don't build your bedroom there!!

There was a priest in the Philippines who visited his people when they were sick and in hospital. In order to help them, he would ask them, to tell him where their cat liked to sleep. This was just his way of finding out if that particular person was sleeping in an unsafe place, as this might have been the cause of their illness. If necessary he would then advise them to move their bed.

The cat is man's best friend - he tells you where not to sleep and where not to sit for a long time.

Where does your cat sleep? Besides the fireplace for warmth, but otherwise on your bed or your chair? If your cat has a favourite place, check the place when you know how to dowse!

Dogs, on the contrary, like good ray places and will have a favourite place, if allowed to sleep anywhere in your house. If your dog's bed is however, in an unsafe place, it won't like to sleep there. If you insist that he stays there - he is very likely to develop arthritis or worse.

Give your dog the run of the house and you will know where the safe places are. We have friends whose dog creeps off to the loo and is reluctant to come away from there! Having checked the house, we found that that part of the house is safe. Yet the kitchen, where he is supposed to sleep, is a different story. He often scratches at night wanting to be let out.

Our German Shepherd suffered from bone cancer. He came to us as a small puppy. In Ireland this dog slept in no particular place but wandered all over from one room to the other. During the day he would prefer to lie outside in the rain, than come inside where we were working. He was about seven years old when his elbow began to thicken. By the time he was nine he was so bad that he could no longer walk up or downstairs. Yet, when he came to our present house, which is a safe place, he started to move about again, even ran around the fields. Although his sleeping quarters were no more comfortable than they had been in Ireland. He lived another three happy years.

I spoke to someone at the University in Vienna in Austria where I was trying to find out some more facts about a paper by a medical professor, on a trial he had done on geopathic stress. When I told my contact that not too many people in England believe in dowsing, she exclaimed on the other end of the phone, "But why on Earth not, with us here it is part of our every day life!" Nobody would move even into a flat without having it checked out for geopathic stress. "Dowsing", she said, "is used by us, by doctors of course, by architects and by most other professions".

Anyway, to come back to the paper I was enquiring about. This professor had carried out trials with hundreds of volunteers. When a volunteer sat on a geopathically stressed area for ten minutes, the effect was measurable! Blood pressure, blood samples and other tests were taken before and after. The results were significant. All the volunteers had reacted to geopathic stress.

Would we, with all our knowledge, put our small baby in a place where it would be bombarded with X-rays? Of course not, because we all know they are bad for us.

So, what about the bad earth rays? Because we can't see these rays we are quite happy to put ourselves, our children and our small babies into a place where our systems can be hammered all night by them.

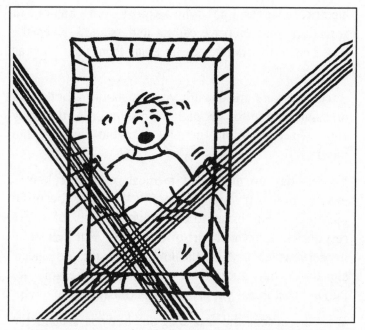

Ask any dowser about cot deaths and they will all tell you the sad story that cot death has a strong correlation with geopathic stress and is a contributing factor, if not the cause of cot death. A tiny baby who has hardly overcome the trauma of being born, having lost its comforting surroundings with the reassuring heartbeat of it's mother. The baby is fed and kept warm all right, but it is in no condition to fight off any harmful rays with its own immune system, nor is it's tiny brain strong enough to counteract the waves of harmful rays.

In many cases a baby monitor is put beside the baby's bed, which means more rays (in this case electric rays) to cause even more confusion to the tiny brain. We do not know, how our brain receives and reacts to electrical waves, so why expose our babies to something that even we cannot understand? Keep the base unit of the monitor as far away from your baby as possible.

Social workers and Health visitors should all attend a dowsing course for geopathic stress in order that they can help even more people to avoid distress and misery.

To this day no doctor or medical researcher knows exactly how our brain works. We have beautiful pictures of our brain to show which parts of it are responsible for which part of our body. But it is still a mystery which part of the brain gives the 'go ahead' signal for our body to function. We presume we know, but it is not yet proven scientifically.

We fully accept the fact that our body is shaped the way it is and that our looks and characteristics have been inherited from our parents. These are all facts, but again nobody knows exactly why we have inherited some characteristics and not others. But do we question this? Of course not. But, we are so sceptical about a kind of communication within ourselves, which after all is dowsing, and yet we do not want to acknowledge it.

The mind is extremely powerful. We all have had telepathic experiences, and have an 'instinct' for certain things, yet we don't want to trust ourselves!!

I know dowsing is a strange phenomenon, but women, certainly the ones I have talked to, are generally eager to know more about it - so they can help themselves in so many ways.

With dowsing, any rays - good and bad - can easily be checked out. Often, all that is needed is to move the bed a little bit further over, or to the other side of the room. Doctors in Austria and Germany, in connection with Cancer Research, worked together with the help of many practitioners and have proven, that whole streets can be affected by rays.

They found that some streets had black water below the houses on one side. These were all exposed to harmful rays. The other side of the street had no harmful rays and the difference was remarkable. There was cancer or serious diseases in nearly every house on the 'black side'. Yet on the other 'harmonious side' people were healthy and there was no cancer to be found.

The same has been found in apartment buildings where people sleep on the same spot on different levels. If the building was on a geopathically stressed area, most people on the different levels encountered cancer or other serious diseases, yet none was found on any level where there was no geopathic stress.

It is only in Britain, that cancer researchers appear not to know about cancer places and cancer streets. They are therefore difficult to pinpoint, as no official research has been sanctioned or encouraged. Why? I do not know.

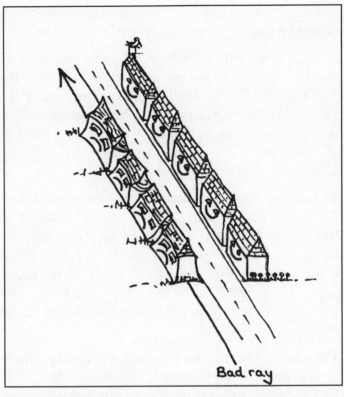

Bad ray

With the blessings of her medical colleagues an Austrian Lady dowser researched thousands of cases of cancer and she never found a single case of cancer where geopathic stress was not present. The same was found with chronic diseases.

What about M.E., migraine, insomnia, learning difficulties, M.S., arthritis and even the feeling of being tired and just not well? The same connection with geopathic stress has been found and proven.

A friend of ours was classified as an M.E. sufferer, not able to work, suffering from depression, without energy, staying in bed for days on end, and the family suffered with him. This man, when he visited us, was 'dragged' to our famous Mr. Thackaberry. The result was, that not only was he sleeping in the worst place in his house, also his chair for watching TV was on the same 'black' spot. His diet also needed a few changes. To cut a very long story short - he had nothing going right for him. His wife made the necessary changes to his diet and moved his chair and bed to a safe position. Now, some years later the same man has completely recovered.

A similar story occurred with a neighbour of ours. A young woman failed to recover from an infection and was treated for all sorts of complaints from stomach pains to panic attacks, looking very ill indeed! She has had medical treatment for over a year and many different tests and drugs, which I am sure did her no good, but all she had to do, was to change the position of her bed and change a few items in her diet.

Yet another friend is suffering badly with arthritis in her hip. She is taking some pills - but they upset her. When I mentioned to her husband before checking out the house, that his wife might be sleeping on water, his answer was, "My wife is not incontinent!" Although we found she was sleeping in a safe place, the rest of their house and particularly the kitchen was badly affected by bad rays. To my mind, this is a typical case geopathic stress.

Black water and harmful earth rays and someone might be sleeping above all this. Many people have a 'feeling' for a place and are sensitive to 'when something is not right' in a house.

When you search the market to buy a new house, you often look at a house and say, "Oh, no not this one, it gives me the creeps". Or, "There was a room I did not like", or "The first house had such a nice feeling despite needing a lot to be done to it - the other houses we looked at, did not have the same feeling".

So the feeling for something right or wrong is there, but sometimes the 'bad' feeling for a particular house will be suppressed, as we get used to it and push that feeling into the background. We make this room into the spare room; fine, mother-in-law won't stay too long. But when we make this room into our children's or our own bedroom that leads to trouble. For eight hours at least we give the bad rays a chance to hammer our system unabated. Night after night. It might take some time before we notice anything, but the body gets seriously affected if we stay in harmful areas for too long. If we are being treated for a complaint, and no treatment seems to work, and there is no improvement, we should at least consult a dowser to find out why.

The same applies to our workplace if we are doing a more or less stationary job. The places where the children sit in school can have an effect. The children become tired and irritable and so it goes on.

The important fact is that dowsers can determine geopathic stress <u>before</u> its too late!

Coming back to our old Mill House. When I think back now, I never really liked that house, but at the time we wanted to buy a house in Ireland and our holiday was nearing its end. In fact, it was our last chance, as we had to go back overseas. So within one week the house was bought and contracts signed. I had voiced my reservations but in the end I gave in and listened to friends who said at the time, what a wonderful place it was and what a garden. (It was May and the garden was ablaze with huge azaleas and rhododendrons. It was a rare sight.) Although the garden was nice, my answer was, "If I want a garden I'll make one" - not having the first idea how to go about a task like that in those days. Looking back at the photos taken before we did anything to the house, it looks grey and cold.

The fact that the house had been on the market for a long time before we bought it, and that no-one had wanted it, was another indication that something was not right. The local people knew about its history and were certainly not inclined to move into such a house. Only somebody as blind as we were would fall for it. Had I been able to dowse, there would have been no way we would have bought such a property, however attractive its surroundings. However, later on we tried to minimise the effect of the geopathic stress - which changed the 'feeling' of the house to a good one! It is now used as a holiday and guesthouse - no better use in it's setting!

As a baby our eldest son would not sleep in the children's room. He cried night after night. We thought it was the change from his old home, and were blind to all the facts which are now obvious. I was pregnant again and feeling very tired. Yet night after night I had to sit and read Peter Rabbit, by which time I had had enough of Peter Rabbit!

Not only did that side of the house have water underneath and bad rays were affecting it, also the house was very old and may have had an unhappy history as well.

Obviously our son at the age of two years old must have felt very uncomfortable - why did he cry for so long, when all his other comforts were looked after! Dowsing could have told me!

Dowsing for one's own purposes can help you and your children in so many ways, it can clarify so many uncertainties and most problems in life are much easier to cope with. You can keep you and your family healthier and happier with very little effort and no extra cost!

CHAPTER 10

I have for many years watched people jogging along the roads, the beach, highways and where ever else they jog. I saw three people jogging on the road early one Sunday morning. In fact, it was two; the third one; an unfit, exhausted looking girl was being pushed along by the two men. Surely, the girl was not up to the strain!

Many joggers look uncomfortable, trying to push their bodies to do something which is obviously painful. I know all the reasons to encourage personal training, jogging and workouts. I am the first one to agree with the concept of keeping fit. But is this particular exercise the right one for you? And is it good for you?

I have tried various exercises myself, from running on the spot, jogging along the riverbank and back (from which I came back more and more exhausted) to aerobics. None of these exercises were suitable for me personally. I have now found a short exercise regime - ten minutes every morning which suits me, keeping me fit and not exhausted, which after all is the point of doing exercises.

If you want to make sure that you are doing the right thing, write down all the different exercises and exercise regimes you can think of. Dowse over them, when you know how to, with the question, "Are the exercises good for me?" and a second question, "Will my body benefit from these exercises" and, "Will I keep fit that way?" The answers will, I am sure, surprise you.

After you have found your right exercise, ask again, how many of these exercises you should do. It is best to write down numbers from one to one hundred, in the case of dowsing a number, the same applies for the 'how long' question. During the course of this book, you will learn how to dowse for the 'how long' and 'how many' question. If the pendulum does not give a clear answer, you then have to find a combination which will suit your body. It is fun to put together one's own personal trainer!

Many people take part in demanding sporting activities, which requires them to be in top form. Dieticians work out the best food regime for weeks and days before the event, including liquid intake, vitamins and minerals. If you now want to make sure that this regime is right for you, you have to dowse over your own diet. You ask your pendulum the question "Is it the correct diet for me for such and such event?" Make a list of all the recommended food, drink, vitamins and go over it, to see whether it needs adjusting for your body. The same can be done with your training. Find out how much training you should do every day leading up to the event. This does not mean that you will be the winner, but it means that you will have done your best for yourself. What a boost!!

I know of people who are told to stick to a particular exercise regime following a heart attack. I am sure the exercise regime is correct, but if you work in a stressful job, would it not be nice for you, just to check it out for yourself. Are you doing the right exercise or relaxation? Which is the best for your physical and mental well being, without adding undue stress to your already stressful life?

Dowsing will confirm this for you!

CHAPTER 11

Many years ago in Ireland we had a visit from Christopher's tutor and his wife from his student days. Both looked remarkably well, travelled a lot and were mentally extremely active. It was very unusual for people of their age to be so fit and interesting to talk to. I asked them "What is the secret, that both of you look so young and healthy and show no signs of ageing inspite of being in your late seventies?" The answer came straight back without hesitation, one word only "Happiness". Well there it was, happiness. I thought about this for a long time - why are there not more people like that? Happiness, is it all self bestowed?

I knew where this couple was living. There was no geopathic stress in either their work or home place at that time.

Surely one constituent to happiness must be health. Anything wrong with our bodies, such as pain, irritation or even just feeling tired is not only irritating but takes our attention away from things which are important to us. There are of course exceptions to the rule.

I have met people, who in their own circumstances should have been absolutely miserable - but yet they smiled and said "Oh, life is far too short to indulge in misery". If most of us would think that way, stress would not affect us so much. Happy people can cope with stress much better than others. Many people work much better under some stress, and provided we don't put our body under any extra stress e.g. geopathic or food stress, we should be well able to cope with the added pressure.

As we have seen, that to be in a geopathically stressed area for only ten minutes can be measured, and it has been shown, that we can be badly affected by it. Our mood changes and our body has to spend its energy fighting 'the intruders' with the result, we become tired and irritable.

Does Britain have more harmful rays than other countries? No, I am sure that this is not the case. Why is it then, that we seem to experience so much geopathic stress everywhere? Geopathic stress occurs naturally all over the Earth, some areas are worse than others but generally speaking there are just as many harmonious areas. It all can be checked out before these are being used.

In our towns, the so called 'good sites' were used up very quickly in the past. In some cases during Victorian times pieces of land which were thought to be unsuitable for other buildings, were then used to build workhouses. Once these had served their purpose, some were either converted into prisons and others in to hospitals. In our days, the same sites are cleared and used for housing estates. The buildings might change, geopathic stress does not!

Unfortunately, we are not always free to choose our own house site. There are many constraints on planning permissions for virgin land outside town borders. However, there are plenty of harmonious sites, and farmland is no longer so precious for our food production. More places should be made available for the needs of our increasing population. It might be some time for things to change, but of course there is us, the people. If we object strongly enough and care enough for our families and our own well-being, we can achieve more than a change!

We went to an home improvement exhibition with the intention of finding a way of advising people about geopathic stress before they buy a building plot and before they start building.

To our astonishment we found that in the whole of Britain, there were 4,300 sites offered for private building. Most of them had derelict dwellings on it. But, none of the counties with available sites offered much of a choice to the individual.

What about people who would love to build a house of their own needs and imagination? Regardless of their social standing. I saw building plots of only 0,125 acre as a house site. Children couldn't even ride a bicycle around such a site with a house on it. If the above figure of available house sites in Britain is correct, it shows a very sad state of affairs. At the exhibition there were many more people on that stand offering building sites, than on the others trying to sell home building needs and services. On the continent the same number of building sites available would be normal just for one county!

Why do planners in a democratic country allow so little personal freedom? Cramped housing estates must be more pleasing to the planners eye, than tastefully developed suburbs with gardens, trees and lawns in between the houses? At least children would have some room to grow up and not being treated as a nuisance because of lack of space, with all the consequent social problems. If planners were to use dowsers or could dowse themselves, then there would be no problem to decide what should be built and where. The guidelines could then help to build on safer places instead of hindering the individual in their choice.

There are so many little pockets of uneconomic farmland, which even with houses on it, could look very attractive in the countryside and still preserve the overall look of the charming way of Britain. The architectural style of the houses do not have to stand out like a sore thumb, but could harmoniously be surrounded by trees and gardens, and hardly be noticed. But, unfortunately we seem to be ruled by bureaucrats, who do not seem to have a human face.

The old council houses have more space around them than some of the new private houses being built; not to mention new housing estates, where there is no room for the children but the road. The planners could easily insist for such projects to have a few houses less on the estates. This would give children more room for either a playground or enough space to play in the confines of their own garden. A few park like areas between all the boxed-in houses would certainly do no harm instead of all the adjacent bare land which very often turns into wasteland.

We live near a small country town. When I look at the new housing estates here, not only do they give me the creeps, but if I did not know where I was, I would think I was in a big town development with no space. Why do the bureaucrats, who have so much power, have so little foresight and compassion?

CHAPTER 12

The recognition of Feng Shui here in Britain will, I am sure, make many Chinese smile. In the Far East it has been a way of life for thousands of years and here we are still wondering whether we should accept it, as there is no scientific proof!!

Do our children have to grow up in unhealthy and unhappy aggressive surroundings? Is that really what we want for them? We, as a society, do care enough to listen to their courageous stories on telephone help lines, but we can offer little help. If they are not happy, what future have they got?

I am appealing to the women, so they will learn to rely more confidently on their own intuitions.

When you make that next move - make sure you are moving to a safe place! If you are lucky enough to have found your own house plot, get it checked out by a dowser before committing yourself! Not every house or street is affected by bad rays - you just have to find the right one.

There are ways to eliminate geopathic stress from an area but I am afraid this is not for the novice dowser.

However, there are ways in which we can avoid the geopathic stress. If there are any harmful rays or water under our sleeping or workplace - the answer can be simple. Move and move as fast as possible. That means move the bed, often by a few inches. Partners sleeping in the same big bed can find that one is the target of harmful earthrays while the other sleeps in a perfectly harmonious place. So, move the bed by whatever distance necessary to be safe. The same applies to the workplace. If it is an unsafe one and the person affected is more or less stationary during working hours, move the desk, chair or whatever! If you find that your house is not a particularly safe one, there are still two options. Move house if you can, but that takes time and is not always possible. There is however, an electrical neutraliser which works well.

My own grandson has one of those neutralisers in his bedroom and he now sleeps peacefully through the night. The little boy is only eighteen months old and certainly does not know what has changed his sleeping habits! For over a year he cried every night for hours on end. The parents were at their wit's end and were just about to consult a children's psychologist.

Another neighbour has a five year old who was going through the trauma of bedwetting on a regular basis. A small neutraliser was installed in her bedroom and Mum can hardly believe that the days of endless washing sheets are over. The reason was, that her bed was and is in a safe place but when she woke up at night, she had to cross a geopathically stressed line, to reach the bathroom which she instinctively could not do, so she wet her bed.

When our boys were small, one of them always lay against one side of the bed, and the other one would never stay in his own bed. Having dowsed over the plan of that particular house, we now know why!

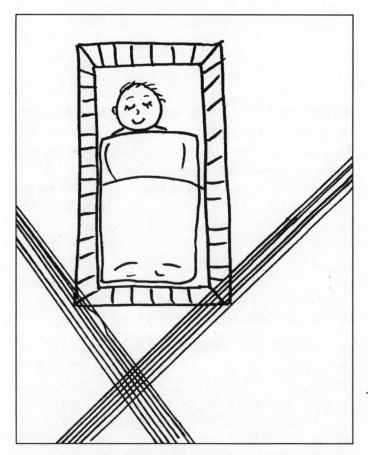

I hope it is now obvious that children who sleep in the wrong place, will try to escape what is bad for them. However, geopathic stress is a very complex area and a professional dowser, who specialises in geopathic stress, should be consulted for a long term solution.

CHAPTER 13

A good friend of ours who was leaving Ireland wanted to buy herself a bolthole in the form of a small cottage. This was not so easy, as even in Ireland most derelict places had found an owner. One day, our friend arrived excitedly at our house and said, "Please, please come with me and look at this sweet cottage, it sounds just right for me". She had heard of this place, but had not yet seen it. Off we went for an inspection. It was at the end of a lane, down two fields, surrounded by an old stone wall, which had been white washed, idyllically placed in rolling countryside. She seemed to have found her dream place.

The ground was rising towards the end of an overgrown garden and wall. Outside that garden wall we saw some pylons. Our friend went scrambling up the bank, leading to the garden wall, to see what else was outside. In the meantime, I looked around the little cottage. My husband was half way between us when he saw our friend collapse, clutching her head. She had to be assisted back to her feet, her face a picture of shock and horror.

The pylons were much nearer than we could see. The wires hung down, creating a strong field of electricity towards the rising ground she was climbing over. She certainly did not need a dowser to tell her if the place was safe!!

The next danger we deluge ourselves and our family with is electro magnetic waves, yet another wave which cannot be seen, but has been found and proven harmful, if we allow it to encroach our lives.

In our old Mill House the electric wiring was not quite as ancient as the house, but we knew there was a leakage somewhere. Yet, it was not possible at the time to have the whole house re-wired. We had trip switches fitted, but had to remove them as they tripped constantly.

There was a time when there were a lot of powercuts, and it is with hindsight that we now can see why we felt so much better when the power off. As soon as it came on again, even the children would remark - "Oh, what a pity, it felt so much nicer without it".

Just because we can't see them, does that mean that they are not there? Well, they are all around us, masses of them in different strength and frequencies, hammering our brain cells and all our other body cells, and we can do little about it. Our immune systems are not used to them, we have had no time to adjust our bodies to fight them off, yet they are on the increase daily, these electro magnetic waves.

What are they and how do they affect us? Well, most of us know that living near big pylons is not very healthy. Many people claim that their health is affected by the pylons and their wires, but this is denied by the officials and electric companies. If however, you can dowse, you will know what the heavy electricity wires do to you and to your children's health.

Electricity is transported from one part of the country to another along these huge pylons with their numerous wires hanging from them. Unfortunately, a high percentage of electricity is lost on its way. It's like a porous water pipe when a lot of water goes in one end, and only a dribble arrives at the other end. The metal in the wires resists the flow of electricity; hence the loss. An electro-magnetic field is generated around the wires. It is said that this can be strong enough to light up a fluorescent tube held below it. This field stays within a certain distance of the big wires, but it has no good effect on us.

It is not only electricity that we have to encounter but there are also electro magnetic waves from radar, mobile phones, TV and radio. We are being scanned not only from the Atlantic to Russia and back, but also down from satellites and back as well. These waves are of different length, and we are exposed to all of them.

All right, we can't see any of them, so we think they can't be there, particularly when we feel safe in our homes. But I am afraid the technology produces these waves so efficiently, that they are everywhere!

Not all of us can dig a big hole and hide, but we can contribute a little to avoid more than necessary exposure.

We are thrilled that we can watch TV and keep our children occupied with computer games and listen to music. We can phone anybody anywhere at any time; we can cook our meals in a microwave oven in seconds. When the microwave ovens first came out, there was a story of a woman who put her wet cat into one of them just for a short time to dry out! Needless to say what happened.

When cooking in a microwave oven, it cooks from the inside out. Think, what prolonged microwave exposure does to our sensitive cells and brain function. Yes, it is safely shielded, but do we know for certain? We can't see the straying microwaves, and we have to trust the promises of the manufacturers. But, if you were to dowse you would know for certain! Obviously faults can occur, and we don't notice if an appliance is faulty unless it breaks down. Keep your children away from staring into the microwave oven door to watch their food going round. A safe distance is at least three feet away, this is advisable for everybody.

The same applies to the TV. Let your children watch only from a safe distance - that is, at least five feet away. Right in front of it, it acts like an electron gun, especially if it is an older model. Although the effects cannot be seen immediately.

Older children, who are hooked to their computer games, are very difficult to convince to stay at a safe distance from their screens. The cables to the playstations are long enough provided they use the whole length.

A few potplants around your living space, and in particular near the TV, will help to 'soak' up the immediate waves. If you have no plants - try and get some. They are not only doing 'a job' but will cheer you up as well, give your children an interest, and maybe, you will start a new hobby - who knows! It is better to get foliage plants then flowering ones. Foliage plants keep longer and are easier to look after, usually they come with care instructions. And, the bigger the plant the better. They do mop up a certain amount of disturbance, especially the ones which thrive in bad ray areas. There is a list of plants in the back of this book which will help you choose them. Don't just have one plant, have several in a group on the floor near the television.

The neutraliser I mentioned before (not available in shops) can also help to reduce the effect of electro magnetic waves. Although there is a cost involved - compared to being ill - the cost is no option!

It is more complicated to eliminate heavy electro magnetic stress from outside. The more trees, particularly evergreen trees, you have around your house the better. When you have some dowsing experience you can confirm all this yourself. If there are no trees near you, plant some in your garden. If this is not possible contact your council to persuade them to plant trees near you wherever possible. In our area the council has just re-tiled the rooftops on many houses. Our neighbours confirmed that their roofs were not leaking. Just imagine how many trees could have been planted instead. Never mind, this is not the purpose of this book.

To sleep with any electronic equipment in your bedroom is an invitation to trouble! Keep it out of your bedroom, particularly portable phones and electronic clocks. If you have a TV in your bedroom, switch it off at the wallplug at night, and avoid BBC aerials. Having had many a sleepless night in hotels I learned why! Unplug TV, aerial and telephone and whoopee I can sleep!

Yes - we have a mobile phone, and I am glad of their existence. It is very interesting when you can dowse, because we were able to check out all handheld units before we bought one. Some are much safer than others, so this is a precaution well considering. It is not what the manufacturers tell you - they, after all, want to sell you something. You have to dowse over the phones and ask your pendulum which unit is safe for you to use.

We are fortunate in that we can re-charge the batteries outside our house, this may not be possible for everybody, but, do it where there is the least exposure to you and your family, in a room which is not in constant use for instance, as transformers can be another hazard and disturbing influence.

Portable phones in our homes, are however, much more upsetting because of their transformer, although as mentioned before we may not feel the effects instantly. We have a friend who is a vet, and very much more tuned into the animal world than today's technology. This man had a portable phone on his bedside table. When he complained to us about headaches in the mornings, Christopher went to check out the room. The problem was the phone of course, which was difficult for our friend to understand, as there were no 'sad eyes' looking at him from the phone! However, he did replace it with an ordinary phone and suffered no more headaches in the morning!

We went to a friend's wedding in Kent. We stayed in a very pleasant place with a view of countryside, fields all around and a few trees here and there. It was a happy wedding and as we were rather more involved than just being guests, we fell into our beds the first night very tired, feeling how nice to get a good night's sleep! We actually had checked the room for water deep down and that was OK. In this pleasant country setting there was no way that we could think of anything but a good nights sleep. After the first night I woke up with a muzzy headache. Well, perhaps it was caused by stress from work, travelling and maybe starting 'flu. It was only after both of us were awake for half of the second night, suffering from severe headaches, that we started to look around. Yet nothing to be seen. When we enquired at breakfast - "Oh, yes", the owner said, "there is a telephone booster antenna in the neighbour's yard, hidden by trees". That was it, we were off!!

We had a similar experience in Cornwall. We were married in Cornwall and thought we'd have a long weekend in the same hotel where we had had our festivities some twenty-five years ago. The weather was perfect. We sat on the hotel's terrace enjoying the sun and the view over the sea with boats everywhere, and it was just what we had been looking forward to - magic!

Suddenly there it was again, the sudden sharp headache and another sleepless night, for no obvious reason. When we enquired, if there was a TV mast anywhere, we were told "Yes, there is a radar installation on the Lizard". Apparently it's huge.

In both cases we had to curtail our stay. We are more sensitive to any electro magnetic waves due to our dowsing, but just imagine what these waves do to our children with their developing brains and constant exposure. The least you can do, is to protect them even if it is only a little at a time.

If you are in the process of buying a house, do look around to see if there are any pylons or any hidden small transformer stations, or booster antenna for TV or phone.

For a short while, we lived in a farm courtyard which was converted into several houses around the yard. At first, the house which we rented dowsed all right for water. It was only after some time that I again began to suffer from constant headaches at night. When it got worse, we began to explore the surroundings. There was no water under the house, this we knew. We dowsed that there were electro magnetic waves coming from one definite direction, but it seemed to cover a wide area. We went further afield to find what it was. We couldn't find anything. It was only when we looked around the courtyard, there it was - the whole area of the courtyard was encircled on three sides by power lines. The courtyard was small and enclosed and we were in the centre of a loop of powerlines.

We then found out that in every house except one, people were suffering from different complaints. I did not want to dowse into others people's health unasked, so I cannot say if their health problems were connected to the electro magnetic waves, but they all said, they were well before they moved there. One elderly lady certainly suffered much more after she moved into one of the houses. Needless to say, we moved out as soon as possible.

When buying a house, do check the area for those heavy overhead cables and look for camouflaged transformers. Try to find a house at least half a mile away from big pylons, if possible with evergreen trees between you and them. The official distance is, of course, much less but to be on the safe side it is better to give them a wide berth.

As you drive along the motor way, there is another source of electro magnetic waves, the boosting or relay stations for mobile phones....just a mast with a few antennae. My husband can tell where these are when blindfolded. "Ouch, there is another one!" It gives him physical pain in the nerve between his jaw and ear. So again, this may not be the sort of 'tree' to have planted near your back fence.

Many of our houses, and certainly most offices and shops, have strip lighting with fluorescent bulbs. Although they serve a purpose, these are particularly bad. The emissions cause a lot of discomfort and disturbance. How many people have I heard saying, "Oh, please switch that light off!" People complaining about headaches, irritability and tired eyes should be taken seriously.

We now live in the heart of the country. Even around here there are people presumably radio hams who put up huge aerials and transmitters in their gardens. It all adds to the fog of electro magnetic waves enveloping us.

What of the lower strength cables piping the electricity into our houses? These are generally not the problem, it's the machines we run off them - TV, microwave ovens etc. But, if we use commonsense we can minimise the problem. Keep the electronics out of the bedroom. Keep the kids some distance back from the TV and do not let them press their little faces against the microwave oven, watching their supper being zapped! Put a few plants around and check with your pendulum that everything is as safe as possible around you.

CHAPTER 14

We should not sleep on water, but why then do so many people go on a beach holiday? Well, I am sure it is to catch a bit of sun. But, to my mind there is an underlying reason.

Most of us are attracted to moving water. The sea or any river - we find it relaxing. We are drawn to moving water, we feel safe there. Moving water discharges geopathic stress and electro magnetic waves. Subconsciously, this is our rescue. There seems to be contradiction? No, there is not. Deep subterranean water has a different effect from that of surface water.

Learning difficulties seem to be hereditary but is this the only cause? Our youngest son is dyslexic. Searching up and down all the families and relations nobody is dyslexic. Is it then one of those hidden genes which only comes to surface in the right circumstances? The right circumstances in this case would be geopathic stress. By all accounts it seems so, because the many books and papers written on dowsing and health mention that learning difficulties can be associated with geopathic stress.

The Primary school, which he attended was not a safe place nor was our home the Mill House, especially where he was sleeping. For years, he would instinctively do the right thing. After school he would take the raft, later the canoe, and disappear down the river, dogs and all. An hour later he would return calm and relaxed. To this day to be near or on water is very important to him. He is the one in the family who tends to follow his instincts more. Lucky escape.

"Keep it simple," an old dowser told me. Dowsing, however is simple, not bound by any rules or regulations and there is no hierarchy. It is you alone, who can ask questions. There is an answer to any question you will ask. The only drawback is, if you don't like the answer, you will have to live with it!

As I said before, anybody can dowse, provided they have an open mind and are willing to forgo all their pre-conceptions. There is no logic to dowsing and the results will surprise you. As we have found many times!

Any wishful thinking will of course, influence the answers. Therefore you have to start with simple exercises until you've gained more experience.

You need something which will serve you as a pendulum. I use my necklace with a piece of amber on it, which has some weight. Other dowsers use an official pendulum, but anything will do, even a piece of thread with a ring on it! When you have gained more experience, and you do not want to be observed in a shop or supermarket, you can use a keyring attached to something which will swing.

All you have to do to begin with, is relax, be calm and ask the right question. Surely this is not difficult? The less you know about the subject you are going to ask, the better. If you already have an opinion, try to discard it!

Never say "Oh, I can't be bothered," or "it's too late," or something else .... give it a try and you will find out!

Once you begin to dowse yourself and you want to know about your health, please don't ask if you or anyone close to you has cancer. You will get a straight "Yes", as all our bodies, even the healthiest contain cancer cells, but they only develop in certain conditions and if your immune system is intact - the cancer cells are dealt with anyway.

The other mistake which is easily made, is that if you are dowsing on behalf of your baby, don't wait until the baby cries. By then, as a mother, you will be anxious and the dowsing will not work.

With a little bit of experience, not only can you improve your own and your familie's health with the correct diet and find a safe place to sleep, but you will be able to lead a happier life, as so many uncertainties will disappear.

With the pendulum, you get three answers: "Yes", "No" and a neutral which means " Whoops" - "I'd better rephrase this question". Your question has to be asked in such a way that you can get a simple "Yes" or "No" answer. Should I plant a rose here? "Yes" or "No"? If the swings do not give a decisive answer, maybe the rose should go to a place nearby or it should not be a rose. Interesting to find out. It is best to ask all your questions during a quiet time during the day, but don't wait until you are tired, you might get the wrong answers!

Ask the right question and the pendulum will not lie. Do not however, ask questions about other people's health or any other of their affairs, unless they have asked you beforehand and you have their agreement.

If you think, oh well, it does not matter, as they won't know, you might find out something nasty, which might not be known to them. What do you do then? Tell them, and risk a row or loss of friendship or worse? You may mean well, but it is better to stay clear from such enquiries unless asked. The same applies to all private affairs of friends and relatives.

There are no rules in dowsing, but if you dowse on behalf of others without permission, there might be unpleasant consequences for you. Always think, how you would feel, if somebody did that with your private life! Of course, if you want to wish somebody well - that's a different matter. By the time you have reached the end of this book, this will all fall into place!

Dowsing won't work with Lottery numbers, although, I am sure you will try. Many people have. If it would work, dowsing would be better known!!

"Why then have we never heard about this dowsing"? I am often asked this question.

There are books, but they are mostly on a specific subject, or they are field studies and not easy to get hold of, it is mainly word of mouth which will pass on the knowledge of dowsing. TV cannot produce convincing programmes on dowsing because 'tests' in public won't necessarily work. Some of the televised dowsing increased public scepticism. So it really is just word of mouth.

If you have taken to dowsing, however convinced you are, please do not go public. Only an experienced dowser who knows what is involved, should attempt such a task. He is then able to dictate the conditions under which to dowse in public.

If you were fortunate enough to demonstrate your ability to other dowsers, - the effect will be positive. However, if you are surrounded by sceptical people, this will produce a negative effect.

Another word of caution particularly to the novice and over enthusiastic dowser. Not only should you avoid appearing in public, but also be careful about wanting to show people that dowsing works. I myself, have witnessed a number of times, that dowsing does not work in public, including TV. It is hard to relax our minds, and to be in our 'own little world' for intuitions to flow. There is an increased level of excitement in front of cameras, lights and transformers. Don't consider it, however tempting. If somebody else is physically near you, that person can influence your dowsing. Too much scepticism or negative thinking has a detrimental effect.

There are a lot of sceptical people and if you talk about dowsing you will discover this for yourself. However, a healthy scepticism leads to discussions, which are always interesting and informative. It is sad when scepticism closes off the mind of a person. When discussing dowsing I have found that it is very often men who find the idea of dowsing, unacceptable. I would love to know why they feel threatened or what they have to fear? Would it be a sign of weakness to be seen to agree with a woman's intuition?

CHAPTER 15

I love houseplants and have a number of them scattered around. With plants it is the same as with the animals; some thrive in bad ray areas and others need to be in a good ray areas to grow, which I did not know or had even considered. Only when one of my plants started to curl up for no reason did I check it out. They were well cared for, did not suffer from either too much water or too little, and they were fed on a regular basis. Yet, the same plant grows and its doing well in a friends house, which I know is geopathically stressed.

When you dowse over your plants or the ones you are thinking of buying find out where in your house they would like to be.

If you are fortunate enough to have a garden, however small, you can plant it to it's best advantage. Your pendulum will tell you which plants will thrive and where to put them. There is a lot of fun and satisfaction in designing or re-designing your garden that way. Bear in mind what is important to you: colour harmony, trees, shrubs or flowers, something flowering all year, rare or common plants, which vegetables to grow this year?

Gardening and dowsing go well together and can save you a lot of work and disappointment.

"Should I plant out these cabbage seedlings today?" If the answer is "No" don't even attempt it. You will soon know why in a very short time, what would have happened if you had done so! Complicated? Not really, once you know the right questions to ask.

I am not a gardener, and I do not have time to spend hours weeding. To me a garden, has to be simple yet pleasing, as I get a lot of inspiration from nature and from everything which goes with it - the birds, bees and butterflies. · If for instance, you are interested in butterflies, you can plant particular plants to attract them. It is helpful to know beforehand however, if these plants would thrive in your place!· Save disappointment, money and time by asking if, say, a buddleia would grow well in your garden, and which variety of them should you buy. There are several to choose from.

I 'designed' a small area around the house with the help of a garden book and my pendulum, and we are all delighted with the results.

If your garden is already established and you have been wondering why some plants are not thriving despite your loving care, they may be in the wrong place. By dowsing it is easy to check.

As a gardener, you may have a long list of plants that you would like to have in your garden. Now of course you can find out if they are suited for your soil type and if so where is the best place to put them.

Make a plan of your garden. Make a list of the plants you want, then check by dowsing where the plants will do best, <u>before</u> you go with your plant list to a nursery.

You then just have the pleasure of planting the right plants in the right place in your garden.

CHAPTER 16

Foods which are offered to us are very different from what they were when I was a teenager. I remember in the fifties when for the first time some luxury foods appeared in the shops - sweets, cakes, biscuits and different kinds of fruit. Before that, people had to cope with the after effects of the War and food was a survival issue. Chocolate was unknown to me as a child. At the end of the War, I was given chewing gum by an American soldier, and I did not know what to do with it!

Today, the foods on offer are overwhelming and not very good for the weak minded. To put on weight therefore, is more of a problem today than when I was younger, furthermore, not everything is good for your health even when claimed to be by the advertisements.

It is very difficult to lose excess weight as many people know, who have tried different diets, with varying results, lasting for how long? I am sure you know, that to be overweight is not good as far as your heart, blood pressure and long term health is concerned. Advertisements in magazines, newspapers and TV, trying to get your custom (and of course, your money), offer many a quick solution to losing weight.

Do quick methods work? Of course not. But, if you can dowse for yourself it is easy! You will very quickly discover what you should cut out on your food list. Just ask which particular foods and drinks on your list should be avoided in order to make your diet work and to lose weight. Your body reacts differently to items on your food list than that of your friends.

Children's nutritional requirements are obviously different from adult preferences. Children are particularly susceptible to TV advertising and they will clamour for the glamour! Beware!!

It may be that you eat too much sugar, cakes and chocolates, but on the other hand it may be alcohol, crisps or too much extra salt! You don't know until you check it out for yourself.

Of course, once you know what is putting those pounds on, it will be so much easier to lose weight, because you will know why you put it on in the first place.

You can work out your own programme, even work out how many calories you have eaten any day without actually adding them up. And, how much more you can eat that day without putting on that extra weight. The same applies to overweight children. Chips and burgers and soft drinks and crisps, particularly milkshakes in front of the telly - are alright occasionally. Your children won't see the point in living healthier lives unless you encourage them to do so and show them an example, or they may still be too little to know they are being overfed. Do they really need so many pints of milk from the fridge? And what about the sugary drinks? Mothers should know better! Children learn by copying, and who better to copy from?

There is no point in overfeeding your baby, you don't do it any favours. Overweight children have many problems socially, psychologically and health-wise. They are likely to be teased in school and to be reluctant to take part in games and sport, and so missing out on a lot of fun in their lives!

If you are carrying around a few pounds too many, and your children are in the same situation, work out a programme together. As a family, even a diet can be fun!! You should have no difficulty in keeping to your "No's" once you know about them. Dowsing will certainly help all the way.

Another interesting subject is that of vitamins. Should we or shouldn't we take any of the supplements on offer everywhere. Articles in some women's magazines say yes, others say no - How should we know whether we are doing the right thing? You can check this out for yourself. If you decide your body needs extra vitamins and minerals - you must be aware that not every brand will be right for you, so it's worth checking which one and particularly, how many tablets or capsules you should take. The correct dosage, however, will change with the time of the month, year and condition of your health.

A modern problem (which becomes a vicious circle) is when we are under stress and have the urge to reach for that quickie chocolate or doughnut.

Many of us have a terrible urge to eat more under stress. And many of us are under increasing stress in our everyday life, self induced or not - physical, mental or both.

Why do we reach for the sweets and chocs and not an apple?

Thousands of years back, in the so called hunting and gathering days stress was the response to danger. So our instinct told us to grab what ever food was available, and escape in order to survive. Not only that, will we have enough strength for whatever danger?

Bees, to this day, gorge themselves with honey when they smell smoke. They do this so they have enough reserves to fly away and re-establish their colony in a safe place.

Now thousands of years later, our bodies have not yet adjusted to the fact that the stress signal seldom means physical danger. Under stress all alarm signals still go off, and we still reach for the next bit to eat in order to have enough strength for that 'danger'.

It's starting to rain. Your car roof is open - your dry washing is still on the line. Seeing the rain - you rush outside to close the roof or get in the washing. Have you ever noticed, that before you start running, that unconsciously you grab a 'bicky' or whatever is handy to eat, on the way?!

The chocolate and sweet market obviously exploits this situation to perfection for their own purposes. Besides, in a stressed state we want to build up energy and high energy food is the one to keep up the reserves.

Once you realise all this, maybe you will be able to resist the temptations when you are next under stress?

There is no pill or panacea to kill such a desire. A stressed body works at it's upper-most capacity. When we then manage to overload it with the wrong food (i.e. chocolate or fatty foods) there is no way that it can give us the necessary energy for our stressful life.

In any case, chocolate is addictive so if you are under stress you are likely to become even more addicted and stress your stressed body even more. Whereas, to grab the apple would benefit your system more.

CHAPTER 17

For years now I have been checking our own food, including meat. It always dowsed "No" for pork. I do check from time to time but it never altered. I wondered why. Evidently, pigs in the past were given antibiotics to combat disease and Valium to quieten them down, when being transported. Apparently, these practices were stopped. Still my pendulum said "No" to pork.

After watching a programme on rearing pigs in the Britain. I now know why we can't eat pork. It was a disturbing programme, and although we were not told what they fed the pigs with, it was blatantly obvious that there is a high level of disease among pigs which are reared intensively indoors. They are not just fed on processed and concentrated pig food and waste, but the conditions in which they are kept makes it necessary for them to be treated with disease preventative drugs. Although it is reported that they are now given antibiotics of a different strain from those given to humans. These remain in the food chain, and who will guarantee that these antibiotics will not affect us and our children in the long run? When you dowse over your pork, sausages and bacon you will find out.

I certainly no longer have pork on my shopping list! I will find an outdoor pig farmer and check on their meat!

CHAPTER 18

If you are willing to take the steps to learn to dowse you certainly will be rewarded by your findings; on the other hand it will make you much more aware, that we should really care about our responsibilities. If we simply put our head in the sand and say that this has nothing to do with us - how on earth will our children know about life, caring and responsibilities?

Old age comes to all of us faster than we would like, but it is then that we have to live with the world we have created, or better - was created for us if we don't do anything about it.

We make a noise when the politicians do or fail to do something, but do we make a noise when it concerns our family and what we feed them on?? And when we have little choice where to live?

Do we care about all those fizzy drinks containing huge amounts of sugar and phosphates which send our children into a hyperactive state? - and then are told it's good for them! Do we care about drugs being fed to animals which will have an effect on us in later years? We blame everybody else from the manufacturer to the government that they don't do enough for us and our children. It takes so little time to find out, what we are actually doing when we buy all these foods and drinks which promised to be good for us all. Unless we check it ourselves we do not know!!!

CHAPTER 19

Do you know how your immune system works?

We have a whole army of 'munchers' in our body who not only stand guard but also get rid of anything unwelcome. The cells in our bodies standing guard decide who is who. Any 'baddy' passing by, such as a cancer cell, 'creepy crawly' virus or unwanted bug, any of these will be gobbled up by the 'munchers'. That is, if our immune system is functioning to perfection to keep us healthy.

In the winter so many people have 'flu, the virus gets passed on to the next person in a supermarket, office, doctor's surgery or wherever. Let the virus enter our body and our immune system will work overtime and

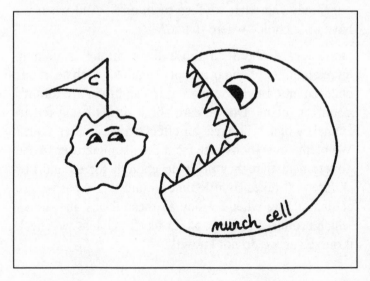

ring all the alarm bells to get 'the muncher's' working. If, for any reason, our 'munchers' army is half depleted and the guard cells are not doing their job properly, what happens then? The 'badies take over unchecked in no time, they multiply and we go down with the wretched flu or whatever it is.

In order to keep our immune systems working well, we need a good night's sleep in a safe place, to eat the right food, light and fresh air with some sunshine if possible, comfortable and non polluted surroundings that enable us to thrive.

If however, for one reason or another one of these conditions is disturbed, then the whole bandwagon is upset. Confirmed trials have shown that our immune system is reduced by half if we get hammered by electro magnetic waves night after night, or sleep on a geopathically stressed area for a long time. I don't have to tell you what will happen! Your body needs all its energy to rebuild its 'munching army', only to find that the next night the same thing will happen again. Eventually we have to exist with a limping army. The intruders are either only partially chomped, or even worse, enter our body unchecked. Then we are in serious trouble. Cancer cells get active, this is the moment they have been waiting for. The viruses multiply and have a holiday in our body. The bugs dance around our guts like nobody's business, while we go groaning into bed feeling very sick indeed. By this time it's too late, we take a few painkillers and gut stoppers, in the hope that we will be alright.

If we don't give our immune system a chance to recover, the feeling of not being quite well goes on and on. It is not my business what adults do to their bodies, if they don't wish to know, but it is negligence and worse, if you let this happen to your children, who don't yet know any better. Their immune systems should be in perfect order. It is up to us to make sure that their environment and their food keep them in peak condition.

When you wear a new pair of shoes for the first time on a day when you have to do a lot of walking or attend a social occasion, you are very likely to come home with a blister. The shoes have rubbed your heel although there was a protective layer between and your skin, not even socks could help prevent a blister. The shoes were such an irritant that your skin reacted. As a consequence you either throw out the shoes or put on a plaster and give the blister a chance to heal. If you keep the shoes the same will happen the next time you wear them.

What do you think will happen when you either irritate your immune system with geopathic stress over a long period of time? The same, your body will react to the irritation at it's weakest point.

The same will happen when we continually eat a 'rubbing diet'. At some point our systems will react.

Unless you remove all these irritants, no way will you give your system a chance to improve. Drugs will do a little or a lot and sometimes make us feel better for a while but if you don't treat the cause of your symptoms, 'the blister' will recur or occur in another place, and the unseen damage of possible drug side effects will go undetected for sometime!

We were sent a diet sheet and a house plan from a lady who has had cancer and now is suffering from Hodgkin's disease. This poor lady has nothing going right for her. She has a big aerial next to her house, an underground stream running through her living quarters and her bedroom seems to be full of electro-magnetic waves. Her diet was not too good either. It is admirable that her system is surviving all this stress. She will be fine if she can move house and change her diet, but will she have the strength to do it? If she had known earlier in her life, all this could have been prevented.

Quite a few people have asked us about Irritable Bowel Syndrome. It sounds a very upsetting and painful sort of dilemma to me. In all the cases that we came across, it was caused by a food allergy. In one case, the sufferer only needed to change three items in her diet and move her bed to the opposite wall which apparently was no problem. She has been fine ever since.

None of the cases had any one 'irritant' in common. So if you are unfortunate to suffer from this complaint get your diet checked over by a dowser. You can't lose!!

CHAPTER 20

Pasteur, a French scientist who lived from 1822 to 1859, spent his short working life on research discovering that germs cause disease. To this day we pasteurise the milk to get rid of the bacteria. However, on his death bed he said "I was wrong, it is not the microbe (germs causing disease) it is the environment."

If for any reason you should be ill or suffer from a serious or chronic disease, do ask your doctor why and what is causing your complaint. Do not give in until you have a satisfactory answer.

I heard of a young woman who apparently has a serious disease of the gut and has had several operations removing the same. I checked the details of this disease in a conventional health book. It stated, that this particular disease was an allergic reaction in the gut! There was this young woman suffering from an allergy which might have had a chance to be cured.

Did anybody find out why her gut was inflamed? How did she get in to this condition? Did anybody enquire about where she sleeps or what she eats? If it is you - do not give in until you have a satisfactory answer!

To have your own peace of mind in any serious case - seek the advice of an experienced dowser. Find out if anything else can be done for you. Once it's 'fixed' by major surgery, it is irreversible.

I am not attacking the medical profession, they are doing their best to eliminate pain and discomfort. I am only saying that if we were more aware of ways to check our health and environment, we would fare infinitely better!

The Chinese traditionally pay the doctor to keep them well, when they are sick they do not pay. Strange? But as a consequence the doctor will try his best to keep them in good health!

CHAPTER 21

Nowadays, being an avid dowser, my allergy to make-up and cosmetics is no longer a problem, now I know how to control them. I still wear eye make-up and put on face creams. I choose more carefully before I buy anything in the cosmetic line, and will dowse the products with the questions "Does this product contain anything I am allergic to?" and "Does this product contain anything which would harm my skin?" The answers are always fascinating. Colourful cosmetic advertisements give you a good chance to try your dowsing at home. Just put your finger on either the picture or the name of a particular item, and ask the question you want to know. Cosmetic products which promise better, younger skin and good looks have never dowsed well for me. But be careful. As soon as there is wishful thinking that you would like to use a product, it will of course, dowse "Yes" for you. Only to find out when you get home, that you have made a mistake. Dowsing cosmetics may be a bit tedious, but it certainly pays off for me. I know, I have chosen the right product which will not upset my skin, cause any irritation, spots or worse. It gives me a great deal of self confidence and eliminates uncertainty.

We went for a holiday on a tropical beach. Everything you read about the sun, beach and holiday, advises you to use a high sunscreen factor to protect your skin. I have a very fair skin and burn very easily. Browsing through all the suntan lotions before the holiday I concentrated on the lotions with a high sunscreen factor. My pendulum said a very firm "No" to all of them. I could not understand it and was getting a bit upset that I could not find the right suntan lotion. Something made me look to the bottom shelf. There were the lotions and oils with a much lower protection factor. A sunoil with a protection factor of only two dowsed "Yes" for me. I was, even after so many years of dowsing for myself - sceptical. My skin which burns so easily and a sunscreen factor of two?

I was sceptical all right, but did not buy any other suntan lotion. I stuck with my oil. As it turned out, it was the right one for me to buy. The weather was not so very hot and there was a lot of overcast skies. I did not burn nor have a red skin but came back with a healthy tan. I have to admit that I never lie in the sun to fry, anyway. So the oil was right for me. Christopher had a completely different one; he dowsed a sun screen factor of ten and normally fares much better in the sun than I do.

Each person has to choose the right product for themselves and it is usually not what you think would suit you nor has the price or brand name anything to do with it.

I have saved myself a lot of money over the years in buying the right cosmetics, perfume and make-up.

Perfume, of course - is the same story! Perfumes contain so many ingredients that I am sure many a woman will be allergic to one part of it or other. By dowsing over the perfumes, not only do I find the right

114

one, but the one which suits me. Judging from the comments I get, I must have chosen the right one. Not me though - my pendulum.

Lipsticks can give you dry and chapped lips. So what do we do - put on either more lipstick or lipcream which of course may not be the right one either. A quick check before buying a new lipstick and all these problems can be avoided.

Hand cream, bodylotion, shampoo, hair mousse and hairspray - all of these products should be checked out before buying. Hair colour and home perms. Find out, if you should use these products. Will they do any harm? The choice is so vast that most people tend to follow the latest advertisement in one form or another, and don't know what to buy. This does not mean that new products are no good, but they may not be right for you. You and only you can determine by dowsing.

CHAPTER 22

On to another cheerful chapter, and that is one many people will enjoy. It will not only save us time and money, but give us a lot of pleasure and the confidence to do the right thing for ourselves.

Shopping. Much more of a pastime now than it used to be, as people generally have much more time on their hands. The tendency today is to drift in and out of shops. When you see something you like, you might buy it, yet you may not as you are uncertain if it would suit you. In particular, clothes and their accessories. How often have you bought the wrong dress, blouse or jeans? You like them in the shop but bring them home, try on, and - oh dear, disaster. You don't really like it. After a time its put away and hardly worn. You could have spent your money better.

If you can dowse for yourself it's easy. I can't emphasize enough that this is for yourself and yourself only. By holding the skirt or blouse or whatever the item, ask your pendulum if this item would suit you and, a second question, if it would fit you. You might still try it on but, certainly as to the choice of suitability it is a great help to be able to dowse over an item.

There again, it's usually the first intuition. You like such and such but ...You have to forget about the 'but' as this concerns only you and not what other people might think. Preconceptions spoil our intuitions. My friends wouldn't approve of this dress - so what if it dowses OK for you, you will certainly like it.

So whatever you want to buy, in which ever line in cosmetics, clothes, food or even a house, dowsing will help you to find the right one.

CHAPTER 23

Our intuitions, I know, cannot be measured or seen or proven. Still, we should trust them in our own personal life to find the many answers we are looking for.

Preconceptions can be most inhibiting, whoever puts them your way, whether they are friends, family, neighbours or TV soaps. We have to live our own life, and our intuitions will tell us what is right or wrong. Hopefully you will discover a whole new world in your life!

One night we had a telephone call asking our youngest son to do a job the next day. At that time, he was registered with an employment agency to tie him over a waiting period. The agency wanted him to start at 4 a.m. and stay over night. My husband's first feeling was, that he should not do it! No reason, just intuition.

As our son did not ask our opinion, we only voiced a note of caution and did not say "You must not go!" Well, the young man took the job for his own reasons.

He started out at 3.30 a.m. only to find that the vehicle he was to drive did not work. By the time it was fixed, one and a half hours had passed. He hardly got going on the motorway when he was stuck for three and a half hours in a traffic accident! By now he was tired and irritable and not in the best state of mind. A lot of time had been wasted by the time he arrived and people complained that he was late.

It wasn't finished there. Two weeks later, he still had problems with this one particular job. His opinion now, is that it would have been much better not have accepted the job! There it is, first intuitions - sixth sense - our dowsing sense!

I first learnt to dowse in Ireland, although there were no dowsing courses. People who dowse in Ireland are people 'with a gift' and they were busy people.

We were curious enough to try ourselves, and our only option was to teach ourselves with the help of books and a pendulum!

Christopher's first attempt had been way back when Mr. Hill had found water under our house. Mr. Hill left the boys with some metal rods to try out for themselves. The boys also persuaded Christopher to try and to his amazement it seemed to work for him too!

Trial and error - as we did not know what it was all about. The dowsing books are mainly aimed at a special subject - water, health, archaeology, map dowsing.

As you can see, for us it has worked in a very special way, and in very many ways. (There is more if you wish to know!).

To begin your own dowsing choose an undisturbed half hour or so. Stand or sit comfortably, relax and hold what you have decided, to choose as your pendulum. Try a necklace and a ring or anything which will have enough movement to swing around. The ring or stone or whatever you decide, should not be too light in weight but if it is too heavy it's no good either.

Hold this, your pendulum, at the end of it's chain in your left hand between thumb and forefinger, and let it swing freely. Make sure that the chain does not hang down much longer than about three inches or ten centimetres.

Relax your mind, let it drift and don't think of anything in particular, for a little while. Then, say to yourself "Please show me the answer for "Yes" and wait. Your pendulum will after a little while - while you are still thinking of "Yes" start to swing. Either up or down or in circles. Make a careful note of this in your mind. This, from now on will be your swing for "Yes".

You then do exactly the same again, except you ask your pendulum for the movement for the answer "No".

And then, there is the question for the third option which can be interpreted as either "I don't know", "Rephrase the question". In my case it would mean "You idiot, you should know better!"

If this has not worked for you properly, try again later. Don't try too hard the first time. Your brain will have to be trained to use the right hand side. After all, this side of your brain has had a rest for some time! If you try too hard you get the wrong answer and that won't do!

Once you've got an answer for your "Yes" and "No" and "Don't know", ask your pendulum which hand you should use for your dowsing - left or right?

Once you've got these answers, you are off!! The movement of your pendulum will be very weak to begin with. It will get stronger in time, but please don't try and swing it yourself at will, as that would defeat the purpose. You have to trust yourself that it will work.

There are a few fun exercises to test out how good you are at relaxing your mind. Get a friend or a family member to put three or four mugs upside down with something underneath, either a sweet, or any kitchen utensil, as long as it can't be seen. You should be out of the room or at least not see which mug has something underneath. Go over each mug slowly with your pendulum and ask the question "Has this mug a sweet, or whatever object underneath?" Then find out how right you were.

The same can be done with glasses filled with water. One with tap water, one with boiled water and the third with bottle water - or one has a pinch of salt, the next sugar and the third nothing. It does not matter if the glass is half or quarter full. The amounts are not important in this case. What is important is the question: "Does this glass contain tapwater?" Go slowly one by one over the glasses pausing in-between. Give the pendulum a chance to react. If you go too fast, there will be no answer. Second question: "Does this glass contain boiled water?" Again hold your pendulum over each glass with the same question in mind. Providing you didn't cheat and look over your shoulder when the glasses were arranged, you should get an answer. Third question: "Does this glass

121

contain bottled water?" And again go over all the glasses, giving the pendulum a chance to react.

Once you have gained confidence with these exercises, try something more challenging. Again get a family member or a friend to hide an article, which belongs to you, in another room without telling you where. Try and find this article with your pendulum by standing still where you are. Ask the question "Is my scarf in the bathroom?" Pause, wait for an answer. Same question for any other room where it could be hidden. This is quite a bit more difficult and you might not get it right the first time. Try again. Relax your mind and have no preconceptions where the scarf could be. If this question is too difficult, then go from room to room and ask, "Is my scarf hidden in this room?"

If your answer is not correct you have to try again a little later, may be when the children are in bed or your partner is out, as sceptics can influence your mind. We know this happens, as our thoughts are more powerful than we realise, and sceptics as well as well-wishers can have an influence.

You will need to observe a few conditions to get to the right state of mind for dowsing. First and foremost, only ask questions which concern you and your family. Do not ask questions about third persons without their knowledge.

In Ireland when our boys were small, and in primary school, an accident happened which upset the whole community. It was Mr. Hill, the water diviner, who brought some solace to the bereaved parents. The boy's headmaster was a very respected and well liked man in the area, whose small boy went missing one day when the local river was in high flood. This river was unpredictable and could rise extremely fast, and very sadly the little boy got caught in this wild water. Search parties went up and down both banks for two days and nights but could not find no trace of him.

Only when Mr. Hill was consulted, with a picture of the little boy and a detailed map, was the mystery solved. Mr. Hill dowsed over the river on the large-scale map, and found that the boy had been caught midstream by an overhanging tree. The tree had been bent down by the force of the water and could not be seen. When the flood subsided the tree came back into sight and Mr. Hill was found to be right.

Back to your dowsing. Be sure your surroundings are not disturbed and aggravated by TV, loud music, quarrelling children or a sceptic person around you. If you have any animosity toward any person near you, do not even attempt to dowse. It will give you the wrong answers. Also don't try dowsing if you are not feeling well. You are talking to your 'other side of your brain' to do so you need to be in a positive mood otherwise the answers will be wrong.

Don't show off your newly learned skill to neighbours or friends who might be sceptical, as again it won't work. Only discuss your dowsing with someone who is seriously interested and will support you.

Do not however, ask any spiritual questions at any time - always remember that you might end up with a problem which you won't know how to solve!

Certainly do not use dowsing for any clairvoyance, such as talking to past presence's or other entities.

You would like to have answers to your everyday uncertainties and those of your family, and for that dowsing is an excellent means of communicating with your subconscience.

Now, with some dowsing experience you can explore a bit further, especially if you are one of those women who is desperate to have a family. You haven't become pregnant - and I am sure by now you have checked out your bedroom and your bed or wherever you make love with your husband or partner. Is it you or him with the faulty parts? It is now up to you to check why you have not conceived.

By dowsing for yourself, you can certainly find the time of the month when you ovulate and can conceive. With dowsing you can eliminate much of the waiting time and soon get to the cause of your failure to conceive. When you go and see your doctor, and tell him about your own findings, be prepared for some opposition if he/she is not a dowser.

From my own personal experience, I once offered my doctor, who is a personal friend (and not a dowser) a book on a subject he was not too familiar with at that time. In it I had found an answer to a small problem that I had.

I took him a spare copy of the book, thinking that he would be interested in reading it. I still have that spare copy.

CHAPTER 24

In England, we have the British Society of Dowsers. When it was founded its members were mainly military men, engineers and doctors.

Many dowsing books, if not the majority, have been written by men, yet it is men who are the greatest sceptics. In my own experience women find it much easier to accept the concept of dowsing and that it works. However men, with programmed minds feel threatened. A friend of ours, who has a scientific training, felt so threatened by the idea of dowsing, that I thought he would walk out of our house when it was being discussed. Yet his wife, who has an equally trained mind, had no difficulty at all in understanding that there is more to life than science and facts. I know that other dowsers have found the same.

I certainly do not want to threaten anybody or undermine the male status; it may be an image problem, or maybe men feel threatened by an unconventional way of thinking and are only convinced by rational explanations.

This is a pity, because it would help many men both in their jobs and in their everyday lives if they were able to dowse. Maybe not in the presence of other people, but on their own, in solitude. All I can assure you is that dowsing can only improve your life and with a little experience you get 'hooked'. It is so fascinating and rewarding. My husband has long given up worrying what people might think about him. He enjoys going to the supermarket and finding the right foods for us by dowsing. In all these years nobody has ever asked him what he is doing, when he is dowsing over the different food items, yet his dowsing is much more obvious than mine.

By now you should be able to dowse over your food. If not, try dowsing over the food items you have at home, with a list of questions. "Are these baked beans good for me?" - "Am I allergic to any of the ingredients in this tin?" - "Is this bread good for me?" - "Does the flour contain anything which would upset my digestive system?" "Are these tomatoes sprayed with chemicals which will upset me?"

You will learn to ask the right question. For instance, if you dowse over your shopping basket and ask "Is all this good for me?" you certainly won't get an answer. You might have forgotten that there is polish or something else in the basket, but the pendulum won't forget.

You come home upset from work and think "Oh, that so and so, why did he do that to me!" I wish him....whatever bad wish you may send his way. Don't do it! When you are a more experienced dowser it might be very tempting, you know how powerful the mind is. I think the best example of a 'death wish' takes place in the film Amadeus. The bad wish certainly came back to torment the man who was so jealous of Mozart? Watch the film and you will know what I mean.

I think all of us have grumbled about our friends or family from time to time. Don't worry, they will do the same about you. What a misery all around. If you stop moaning and put yourself into a good mood with the help of your pendulum, you will be very surprised at the affect it will have on you! Think positively and you will be surprised to find, how things will change all around you.

As a man, maybe you are not interested in dowsing over the food, or your health. Very well. But, what about "Does my car need an oil change?" "Should I buy this car?" "Is it a bargain?" If you are buying a second hand car, find the section in the autotrader which interests you most. Mark the cars which you would consider and then go over them with your pendulum and ask which of these would be the best buy for you. You can, of course, ask more questions, but don't ask the same questions again and again. Don't ask complicated questions either.

If you buy a new car, get all the brochures and ask which car would be best for you to buy. You won't be disappointed I am sure!

The fact that we lived in Ireland beside a river, with the prospect of moving to a small farm in England, made us decide on a four wheel drive as our next car. The Irish market is dominated by Japanese cars and we really did not know which make to choose. From a list of all possible four wheel drives, we dowsed one that was fairly new on the market at that time. Living in rural Ireland, we certainly were not up to date as to the latest market trend in such vehicles, but the one we

127

dowsed, and subsequently bought, has certainly proven the best one for us. We bought the same make again, for the second time!

Before you go to the pub, make sure you drink the right brew. "Am I allergic to this kind of beer?" - whatever the brand name - Or "Does the smoke in the pub upset me?" - There are certain beers you may not like, yet you drink them because your mates do! Check which one is good for you, and you will enjoy the pub twice as much.

Alcohol is one of the items a dowser would check on one's food list. Under normal circumstances there is nothing to worry about, as an occasional drink - or even a regular glass of wine or two - are good for you and most enjoyable. (If you then drink an equal amount of water a hangover can be avoided or the effects at least minimised). It is usually a smoky atmosphere which gives me a hangover more than the actual alcohol. Pain (in this case, the hangover) is just the body's cry for help. Pain in the head the next day may not just have been caused by the booze mopping up spare water in your cells, but also by the passive smoking. Very easy to check once the head has cleared. But what I want to mention concerns drug and alcohol abuse. The pendulum does not lie, if asked the proper question. If parents are concerned about their underage children, there are ways to find out what is going on. Although this is not for the novice dowser to try, as a mistake can have severe repercussions. Any experienced dowser will be able to help worried parents who are still responsible for their children's lives. When you are no longer responsible for your children's lives - you can only stand back and hold your breath.

Of course, you cannot show off your newly acquired skill or knowledge to the other people in the pub either, if you don't want any leg-pulling. But, in your own solitude try and find out! Be careful however, when you ask about your mates, or even about your girlfriend. It is not your place to ask about them without their knowledge.

Maybe it would appeal to a man to dowse the right holiday for himself and his family?

Holidays are a good dowsing subject and many pitfalls can be avoided - the hassle of getting there and back, choosing the right hotel, finding out about the weather, the food and the water, not to mention the likelihood of getting tummy upsets and wasting time with being sick. You can dowse over your food when you are on holiday, to check those prawns or that salad, or the ice-cream.

Dowsing for your holiday, how do you go about it? First, you look at your calendar and see when you and your family can take a holiday, and when and where you want to go. Presuming you want to go away and you have all the brochures. Spread them all out on a table, relax and start your questions. You may want to write the answers down, so have everything ready.

First question: "Where should I go on holiday during such and such a time?" You then dowse over all the countries or places which you consider going to. If none dowse positive - find another place. This is always the challenge of dowsing - find the right answer!

You then ask, what the weather will be like during that time in that country or place. And after that you can ask, which hotel you should book, again going over the hotels in question.

We have had very good holidays that way with good weather, and everything we wanted from a holiday was right! The last time we actually wanted to book a different hotel from the one we dowsed - it looked and sounded better in the brochure. However when we visited the hotel we thought of booking, we knew straight away why the one we were staying in had dowsed so well for us. Although it was slightly more expensive, there was no comparison between the two. We also had good weather, while islands further north and more popular, had bad weather and storms.

If you go by car on your holiday, get a map out, mark the two points, 1. from where you are setting out, and 2. where you want to go. You then write them down, as well as the day you would like to travel. Go along the map with your pendulum and find out the best route. Explore all the possibilities.

You then write down the anticipated travelling time, and find out when is the best time for you to leave with no major hiccups! It's a challenge!

My family was arriving from Germany, and I was checking what time I should leave for the airport with my pendulum. All it said was "No", "No", "No". I was getting a bit anxious, but waited. Eventually, I got a telephone call from my sister saying the plane was delayed for some time during transfer in Dusseldorf.

The other event, at the same time unbeknown to me, was that the motorway was completely blocked for miles on both sides by a major accident. When I finally left, having checked again, the motorway was free, and

I got to the airport at the same time as my family walked into the arrivals waiting hall.

When we moved into this house, being a new one, we needed a few bits and pieces of furniture. We went to one of those big furniture outfits, chose our lot, put it on a trolley, and returned to the car. We packed the car hurriedly as it was raining but - oh dear! We had bought more than would fit into the back of our car!

We had nothing with which to fasten the packages onto the roofrack. What a dilemma, not to talk about being embarrassed. What to do? We unpacked everything, stood back and thought, well why not dowse how we get this lot in? So we dowsed over each parcel in which order and which way it should go in. In no time the car was packed, every inch was used and we had room to spare!

So when you go on holiday - here's your chance! I often see badly packed cars, with roofracks nearly falling off. Before you pack your car next time, put all your luggage around you, within sight. Then ask your pendulum which piece of luggage should go into the bottom of the boot and which way, then the second one and so on. I am sure the result will amaze you.

CHAPTER 25

Another 'male' subject for dowsing is of course farming. Some years ago, I was listening to the farming programme early in the morning and one farmer said "We, the farmers, are the keepers of the English countryside". Well, you can debate this for a long, time but now it seems that decisions are made according to the amount of subsidies available for which ever crop is planted. Nevertheless, there are farmers who really do care, I am sure, and it's for them that I am writing this. The farmer who is in tune with nature should find it very easy to dowse. In farming there are very many areas in which dowsing could be of great help.

Weather forecasts are very accurate these days and you can get the farmer's weather forecast for a week ahead. However, what do you do if you've missed it, especially if you haven't had time to watch the news in the morning. With dowsing, you will not only know what the weather will be for a day or two, or a week, but with a little dowsing experience you can organise your whole farm life; where to assign your people for what job. It is just amazing how well it all works out.

Your expensive soil analysis, you do it yourself in an instant and when you are doing that, find out at the same time which fertiliser is needed this year. It's not what you think is needed, but what is really needed by your soil. So much better, so much time and effort is saved. I just hope you are not a sceptic. It will work very well, for the ones who want it to work!!

We have a few acres ourselves and it certainly has worked for us. It is well worth giving it a try. Have a map of your farm and, holding your pendulum over the map, ask from a list of crops, which crops you should sow where. With the right questions you will get the answers. The same applies to which fertilisers to use, and if any sprays are needed, at which interval.

Are you giving your animals the right food mixture? If it says "No", you then have the problem of sorting out what is wrong with the food. Have your animals everything they need to thrive in the fields? Shelter for weather that is too hot or too cold? For that reason would it be better to let the hedges grow??

When we bought our tractor and being new to the area, we had no preference as to which make or which agency to choose.

We dowsed over all the possibilities from a list of all the popular makes. The tractor we eventually bought, was relatively unknown to us but proved to be the nearest agency with the best deal!

As you only get "Yes" and "No" with the pendulum, the questions have to be asked, so that you get the answer of "Yes" or "No". I know that farmers wives will have a job convincing their husbands but I am sure they can convince them somehow!!

Any organic farmer should certainly use dowsing to help his way of farming. So should land conservationists, garden designers, foresters and many other people connected to the outdoor life.

A sheep farmer always has a big decision to make as to when to shear his sheep. I remember in Ireland that every year, when the weather had been fine for sometime, the farmers would shear their sheep, but soon as this had happened, the cold weather was bound to come back! They weren't our sheep, but even looking at them, made me shiver. I could put my warm clothes back on again, but what about the sheep?

An experienced dowser can tell when it is the right time for the sheep to be shorn, without running the risk of their catching pneumonia or worse.

One year, we asked which crop we should grow to improve some neglected land. We dowsed that we should sow borage, the right sowing time and how much seed we needed. It grew beautifully. That summer, most other farmers who grew the same crop lost theirs due to a late frost. We did not, but one thing we had forgotten to ask was, will we be able to harvest the borage. We presumed we would, but, had we asked, we would have known better! But then again, we only had asked how to improve the land, which it did.

CHAPTER 26

We had a friend in Ireland, our big burly guardian angel, who could turn his hand to anything and everything. He was also well known for his capacity of consuming a few beers.

The two men, Christopher and the friend, were painting one of our guest chalets in Ireland, with a new paint. After some time of painting, both men were affected by it - our children had long left the scene, saying that they didn't like the smell of this paint. (Maybe they did not want to be given a job, we thought!) As both men had tears in their eyes, they did not want to turn and look at each other, just in case of being thought of as soft ! The chalets had to be repainted, and it took a lot of beer to dry the tears. The paint was unbearable.

After a cold winter we wanted to double our insulation under the roof in the Mill House. We used fibreglass, the only insulation available in those days, and did not think anything of it. Our burly friend climbed into the attic to lay the rolls across the whole area under the roof.

He was a great fisherman, but we had never seen him going into the river voluntarily - he did not like getting wet. That evening he ran and jumped in! I don't have to tell you why...!

The cause of many allergies, and breathing problems is, of course, insulation materials, paint and wallpaper. I know that some insulation materials can cause asthma and skin allergies. It is just as well, to check before you insulate the attic. It is distressing to find you and a family member react to something contained in these materials. To re-do the whole job again, would take double the time and, of course would be much more expensive and troublesome.

The same applies to carpet materials. It is always better to have a natural material such as cotton or wool, than nylon, which develops static electricity. There again - check - and you will know. A wooden floor with rugs can be very attractive and just as easy to clean as a carpeted floor.

It is well worth checking out all these things, before you have your house painted, your baby's room decorated and carpeted and before you move into your new house.

Some burglar alarms can distress the inhabitants of a house without them being aware of it. Nobody will suspect them though. I certainly can tell, when there is a burglar alarm on and so can Christopher!

At one stage, we were looking at showhouses. I am very interested in building houses, but very often we had to leave quickly because we were experiencing a muzzy feeling, which transpired to be caused by the burglar alarm. I am not saying you should not install a burglar alarm; I am only saying look at all the options, write down all the names and dowse over them. The one which is all right for your neighbour, may not be all right for you.

CHAPTER 27

Dowsing is simple, and keep the questions simple. If you for instance ask about squash - there is more than one meaning to the word, so you have to define which word you mean: to drink, play or eat. So, it is important to define your questions.

I have given many tips in this book that other dowsers may not approve of, but these are important matters in our everyday lives, even if not everyone sees it that way.

When you look at your wardrobe to decide what you should wear for that special evening or even in the morning when you just can't make up your mind, you can ask your pendulum, which would be the most suitable outfit to wear. It is worth while spending a little time over this because you no longer waste time hesitating. How often have I found I wanted to wear something other than what was indicated by my pendulum. Well, every time I follow my sixth sense I am correctly dressed, which I would not have been, had I dressed by just picking out something at random.

Talking about enjoyment. If you are at all doubtful about which particular film to watch on telly or not - just ask!! Read a book - ask which one you would enjoy. Laughter or excitement, joy or heartbreak -it's easy!

Have you ever been in a restaurant, and wondered what to eat - maybe even in a foreign country?

Here is the answer. I very unashamedly take my pendulum and go over the menu. I always find something to eat which will agree with me and which I enjoy. The menu jargon, even in this country, often means nothing to us and we don't want to ask the waiter. If you are hesitant, have a practice run with your local curry or Chinese takeaway.

When we were in Italy one year, we decided we wanted to eat real Italian food. We ended up in a small but very busy restaurant - Italians only. No English spoken!

The menu might as well have been written in Chinese! We hadn't a clue what to eat. We then both dowsed over all the dishes on the menu. When we finally got our food, it was so delicious, we went back there several times!

In the past our dinner parties always seemed to be successful. People would always remark on how much fun the evening had been and I know they were not simply being polite. My best kept secret was, to write down all of my guests names and then find out with my pendulum who would be best seated next to whom. It was just magic how it worked. The most incredible people would get on well with each other, especially those who would not normally choose to sit together.

By now you should have some confidence with your dowsing. If in doubt, write down your list of questions and dowse over them when you are not tired and undisturbed. There is no right or wrong, you only need to find the right answer for you. Hopefully, by now you should have had quite a number of the right answers and you will be convinced that dowsing works. But what about your husband, your mum and your friend? Don't worry if you can't convince them; eventually they will come round to your way of thinking. They will see that you are a different person with new self confidence.

I remember we had once had to explain to a bank manager what we were doing with our land and what we were growing. He turned to me in utter amazement and said: "I do admire your self confidence

- how do you know all that and how can you be so certain?" Needless to say, I did not tell him.

So once you have mastered your initial hesitations, you have probably made a few mistakes, and wondered what has gone wrong. "She is not right after all!" Well let's go over how to ask the questions.

Keep your questions very clear and very simple. Does my daughter like baked beans? Does she like them for what? To play? To throw out? To sit on them? To eat of course - did you say so? The correct question should be "Does my daughter like to eat baked beans? Do baked beans contain anything she is allergic to?

You see, the questions need some thinking about if you want to get the right answer.

Should I go on holiday? Of course you should, so the answer is bound to be yes. Should I go on holiday in July? Should I go to China for my holiday?

So you see how important it is, to ask the right questions very precisely.

I had a nice example. A friend discovered that she could dowse. Naturally, she was very excited. Out came the mugs and I put something underneath one of them while she was not looking. The first time round it worked perfectly, but when I changed the object around and she tried again, it did not work. She asked the question "Is there something underneath this mug?" Well, the mug was on top of a kitchen work surface, so there was the work surface, the cupboard, shelves in between... You can see now, what I mean. It probably sounds tedious but with a little practice it will become easier.

When you are more at ease with your dowsing, write your question down. There maybe several answers possible. As well as that, write down 'Other' as an unthought of possibility. If by any chance your answer is 'other', then you have to think further to find more ways to answer your question! For example: You are undecided where to go for your holiday. List out all the locations you would consider going to: China, South America, Spain, Centre Parcs or 'other'? A challenge to the left hand side of the brain.

With a few successes behind you, you now can explore further and improve on your food lists and those of your children. You may have always wondered why one of your children always eats everything and the other doesn't. There might be a good reason. One child might not like what the other child favours. Find out, and it will stop a lot of agro. You don't have to keep saying, "Hurray up, and eat". You now know what your children like, and the reason why. Let them eat what you have dowsed. Knowing what is good for them will have a good 'knock-on' effect.

I used to get annoyed with myself having to urge my children to eat what they were given - I only wished I had known then! Surely, if we did understand our children better, there would be no need for constant nagging and shouting.

Dowsing will certainly help you to understand your children from a very young age, because it is a very helpful way to communicate with them, to find out their needs and wants. Are children produced to have them put into social care just because some mothers don't know how to cope with them? That would be a very poor way of shedding our responsibilities.

I have worked all my married life. I was lucky in so far, that most of the time I could work from home and I could choose my time and work late hours if necessary, so I had enough time for my children.

I know I was fortunate, and I realise that this is not feasible for most people today. But, how else can you avoid putting your children into someone else's care? What about your mum or another family member?

You can always ask your pendulum to choose the right childminder for your situation. Just ask if your child is missing anything or if it is happy when you are away and "Yes" or "No" will give you the answer. Is it better to give your children a happy childhood, or is it better to pursue a career or can you find a way to accommodate both? There is a way for you to find out. This is a challenge for both left and right side of the brain!

Children have all perceptions at a very young age and it would be nearly punishment for you, to realise later on, that you have missed out the best time of their childhood.

I know a case, of where a small child was adopted and although he did not lack any physical comfort, he always knew instinctively that his adoptive parents were not his real parents. At the age of ten was then told, that he was adopted. His immediate reaction was that of relief. His instinct had been right. That boy is my son.

Children at the age of five have a wonderful intuitive understanding and knowledge of many things be they animals, trees or paintings.

At an even younger age most children have simple answers to their needs, much to the amazement of their parents. "Where do they get it from?" "How do they know?"

Unfortunately nobody takes them seriously, and formal school or religious education puts a stop to all this and it's lost to most of them forever. How can we train our children's minds without programming them? Maybe one day we can find a way to reconcile the two, training and intuition. Dowsing will help you, as a parent, to encourage your children to retain their ability to understand intuitively.

Children with no formal education keep their perceptions alive which has been acknowledged by a well known biologist who went to live amongst those children.

Yet we insist that our children go to school at a younger and younger age.

Why are mothers often so ambitious for their children? Hardly can they walk, before we put them into some form of child minding institution. Mothers who do not go out to work will say "Oh, Johnny has to learn how to mix with other children". Was her Johnny ready for it? Is it not better for your child to be with you until they are ready to mix? The children themselves will know best, and you can check by dowsing.

We certainly made the mistake with one of our boys. "He has to learn to play and behave with other children", I said.

With hindsight, he certainly did not. It would have been much better for him and the whole family if he had stayed at home to play and develop in his own environment. Taking him to a playgroup became a chore, and although he was occupied during the morning he did not gain much 'socially'. To this day, I reckon, he has a feeling of being left to one side. Which of course is far from being the case.

Often children only go to a playgroup or kindergarten because their mothers want them to go and yet they have no idea that the children are just being 'minded'. I have nothing against playgroups or kindergartens. If they give the children a chance to develop, no better place. But, is your child ready to go? Or is it easier to leave the 'childminding' to someone else! It is not what your neighbour or friend tells you that counts, because if that were so, you are just imposing public opinion on your children. Will the same public opinion help you later on, when you have a problem with your child - I am sure it won't. Until the age of five or six, it is so important for us to give our children a chance to develop into their own little world, to develop all their senses and abilities with mother and father helping them.

We should not belittle their ideas and suggestions in front of others. Children's minds have much more to offer than our own at times! They have not developed formal thinking and their ability to see things should just be accepted by us. Children can cope with most things, and will have their own simple answer. There is usually no need to say, "Oh, you musn't tell the children they can't understand that".

I was introduced to my grandchildren by my first name, not to confuse them at a very young age with their fathers adoption and all it's complexities. They took one look at me and said "Oh, you are Dad's sister!" They knew instinctively we were related!

In some countries, formal school education only starts at the age of six and it has been proven that these children soon catch up and overtake those who started schooling at the age of four and five.

Again dowsing would tell you what is right for your child.

It is fun to dowse with your older children. Make up games like "How old is this tree, this house, this car?" Dowse over a map and find old castles, fortresses or stone age sites. You can make a sketch of your garden, hide a coin and ask your children to find the coin, either on the sketch or in the garden, or you can play treasure hunt with several objects!

Make up games of where to find a picnic place in the countryside near you, where and when to go to the seaside. Where and when to go fishing. Your children will tell you. What fun you are going to have when you go and find out who was right!

Would granny like a bunch of flowers today or a box of chocolates? Dowse it, and it will be delight all the way, granny will be pleased, because that is just what she wanted and the children will be pleased because it was 'their idea'.

They go in for a local competition, which section would they enjoy most? It does however, may not mean that they will get a prize! It will help them to shorten the decision time of which section they should enter.

CHAPTER 28

Do you ever go for country hikes or walks, and how often do you wonder which way to take when you come to some cross-roads. If you have taken to dowsing, just ask your pendulum which way to go. If you want to find the quickest way or the most challenging way, or the most beautiful way, ask again.

Before you even set out, decide over a map with your pendulum which part of the country you should see, and, which way will be the best for you to go - keeping in mind what is important to you.

In everyday life or on holiday, if you want to find a specific place, which you simply cannot find, either by walking or driving, just ask your pendulum to show you the way. Please, if you are driving, stop, calm down, and then ask.

I was once completely lost coming off the motorway up North, where I had never been before. A friend had given me incomplete instructions. At a roundabout off the motorway, I went in the opposite direction from where I should have gone. I knew it wasn't right, because the name of the place was not signposted. I stopped and asked my pendulum.

When I finally arrived at the friend's place, and told them the route I had taken, they were amazed that a stranger to the area could have known it. It was a shortcut only the locals would know!

Anywhere you want to go, and want to know the best route to avoid traffic jams or any other hazards, just ask your pendulum beforehand. If it is not your usual route, you might eventually find out the reason.

I dowsed over a sketch of a friends house the other day, where I had never been before. They wanted to know if it was built over water or if there was any other hazards. Although they both had a good feeling for the house, they wanted to make sure. I got a different reaction from my pendulum which indicated something other than water. It was just at the left hand side of the bed, circling over the top half. Christopher found the same. There was no water. So "What do you have on your bedside table?" was the question. "A digital clock and the telephone," was the answer. The reason for some sleepless nights.

With dowsing, we can discover the ability to remove the unnecessary stress in our lives and on our systems. Extra electro-magnetic waves, irritants to our digestive system and irritants to our breathing, skin and general living can be avoided. We can only enhance our lives by removing uncertainties, and solving everyday problems, and with that help ourselves to lead happier lives.

Who then needs pills or potions for a longer life?? It will happen automatically!

Dowsing has been called 'the forgotten language of instinct'. If some of us would keep it alive, we could help our children's lives to be happier.

The survival of this planet would stand a better chance, if we all cared a little more, just by dowsing for our own purposes - every little bit helps, even in dowsing.

People who take to dowsing at a later stage in their lives will certainly not be bored when the time comes to retire. Dowsing needs no hierarchy, no special buildings nor money. It opens so many new avenues, in fact it opens up a new way of life. You will find, when you talk to any dowser, retired or otherwise that they are very busy people with no time to be bored as there is so much to find out and discover. Dowsing over maps, archaeological sites, old churches, dowsing over history books, herbs and their healing power, once you get 'hooked' the list is endless, and your imagination is your only limit.

CHAPTER 29

A very good way to use your dowsing, is not only to communicate with your children or animals, but also with people who are handicapped or who have had a stroke and cannot communicate with us in the usual way.

First you ask, if you are allowed to communicate with such and such a person. If your pendulum says "Yes" go ahead, but if it says "No" leave it until you get permission. In the case of "Yes", ask one question at a time and get the answer. Find out how they are, if they are missing anything that would make their lives more comfortable and what they would like you to do for them. You can find out all this by clearly asking your questions in such a way that you can get a "Yes" or "No" answer.

Not so long ago I had a strange experience in two different locations. I was buying something in a chemists shop, and an elderly woman in a wheelchair was pushed past me. As she passed, she made a lot of noise and pointed towards me; obviously she must have felt instinctively that I would have been able to communicate with her, but she was pushed into the opposite direction. The same happened in another location. In this case, a teenage boy was walking around with his family. He was mentally handicapped. He very much wanted to get in contact with me but again the relatives pushed him away. Obviously, their subconscious told them much more than we realise.

How does a blind person know where to walk safely? They must trust their sixth sense much more, they have to! And it works for them. Why not for us?

When you dowse having had some practice, do thank your subconscious mind for giving you that advice. It will be appreciated. After all, your conscious mind likes to hear some praise as well! - If you never get any praise in your home, or in your job or from friends, you get depressed - the same for your subconscious mind.

When you next park your car in a public carpark and you are worried that somebody might damage it, here is what to do! Before you leave your car, just walk around it with your pendulum in your hand, and ask for it to be protected while you are away. This you can do, not only for your car but for many things in your life, just ask for protection for such and such, and don't forget the 'thank you' afterwards.

With dowsing not only can you find mislaid or lost articles, a lost pet but a missing person.

Don't start on a complicated search for a missing person. This should be left to the professional dowser. You can, however find your own mislaid articles the easy way. Can't find a key? Ask your pendulum but don't forget you have to give a description of what key it is. Don't ask for a key unless you only have one key. "Yesterday, I mislaid my car key, where did I put it?" The pendulum will show you in which direction to go. Follow it and you will find it!

The same will happen, when you are looking for your missing pet!! It will also work if you are looking for a book in the library, bookshop or an address in the Yellow Pages. If you seek some information about gardening for instance, or any other subject, and you don't know where you read it, or where to find it, hold your pendulum over the garden or other books you have, and you will be shown the book containing the information you are looking for. If you are more experienced you can even find the right page!

CHAPTER 30

The one day in our lives, which should be the happiest and most exciting is our wedding day.

I used to do a lot of flower arranging for weddings in Ireland and it was always exciting. Usually the people were happy people, unless mother interfered too much! I always felt very sorry for the young girls who knew what they wanted, but mother said "Oh, no dear, that would not be right" - no reason given!

If either mother or daughter were only able to dowse, they could have saved themselves a lot of arguments and agro and the lead up to the wedding would even be a happier one.

Colours for the bride - white, cream or other - just dowse over the colours and the bride will be glowing in the right colour. Bridesmaids colours the same. There is so much indecision and wondering what would look right for girls with the different haircolours and styles, figures and ages. When you can dowse, this is all no problem at all. You will find either one colour or a mixture to make all the bridesmaids happy.

Your flowers, the food, the wine, and table settings and who sits with whom - what a nice way to arrange a wedding. It will be the wedding of the year, even if you don't belong to the upper classes. You can't of course leave arrangements to the last minute, because there is a lot of dowsing to be done, but then weddings are planned a long time ahead these days and what a change to self confidence after all the uncertainties.

I was asked to arrange the flowers for the wedding of a friend's daughter. The girl was not quite sure what she wanted - she knew but she didn't know - she had too much to think of with all the arrangements and decisions. I finally got her to agree to leave it to me. I am glad she did - her flower arrangements were exactly what she wanted!!

I hope you all remember when you were teenagers. All right - today's teenagers seem to have changed since we were teenagers. I know that today, they have more liberties but I am sure that teenagers reactions to growing up have not changed. Most teenagers are extremely uncertain about their feelings, their looks, their self confidence - not so different from us!

Today's teenagers have more choice in clothes, food, music and socialising. Their need to 'belong' to somebody or to a group is certainly different from my time as a teenager. Maybe it is a national characteristic, that every fashion - whether suitable or not - has to be followed to the dot. Their peer group seems to have a lot of power and influence over them, yet the individual is even more uncertain.

Fashion, music, cosmetics and implied behaviour being marketed not only by young people's magazines, have a strong influence, and we as parents have to put up with it, and seem absolutely powerless.

It is very difficult as a parent to convince one's teenage child against the opinion of the group. Yet there are small things which we can do for them, which might almost go unnoticed, yet are very important to any teenager of any sex. Spots!! If you, as a mother can dowse over your teenager's food. Despite all the junk food consumed - the food you provide should help to make up the deficiencies and improve their skin. Acne, eczema is very debilitating to the self confidence, and usually it is only due to the wrong diet and cosmetics.

Write down what your child eats during the course of a week, and check them out. When you go shopping, don't buy the offending items in future. Buy something else instead, which you have checked out beforehand. Teenagers have enough problems over growing up, and a spotty face does not encourage their self confidence.

When they were teenagers, our children tried some of the face washing lotions advertised. The spots got worse. They don't smoke (which is very bad for young skin). The problem definitely was their diet. It will be a challenge to you as a mother, to find something other than ready made snacks to satisfy their enormous appetites. Many teenagers suddenly increase their intake of - let's say cereal and milk. It may double or even treble. If somebody is allergic to dairy products and their body suddenly has to cope with double the intake of the 'poison', the reaction is bound to be violent, and out come the spots. So, find out what would be good for them instead and feed them accordingly. They will thank you for it!! To have a smooth skin will be the envy of the others, so well done Mum! The same with clothes. You can quietly influence your daughter that a different style and colour would suit her much better than the fashion, - which she only follows because she doesn't know any better!

We have a friend with the most beautiful auburn hair. I know the agony she went through in rejecting a fashionable colour because it would make her face look sallow, yet with the right colour she is stunning. Try to experiment with your daughter. If you are successful she will believe you when you give advice about other matters. And these stressful teenage years can become very enjoyable for both teenagers and parents.

I was introduced to an attractive young woman one morning. Most people do not look their best on a Sunday morning after a party on the Saturday night. This girl didn't have a hangover, yet when I looked at her, something was wrong - suddenly, I could see it - it was her shirt. She wore a white shirt, which made her look very pale, as it was not her colour. She obviously did not know that white does not suit her. If we wear the colours that enhance our looks, it increases self confidence.

I saw the same girl again in the evening, having had an exhausting day, and wearing a rusty-red jumper over her white shirt, which was her colour and what a difference it made!

How do we know which are the right colours to suit us? Dowse over the different garments in a shop and you will find out. If not, dowse over the colours in a catalogue (even though they won't be quite true they will give you an idea) with the question "Is this colour going to suit me?" You may not see it yourself straight away, but your friends will certainly notice.

Your colour scheme in your house - you are fed up with it and you want a change but... there is such a choice of wall papers, different coloured paints and so many samples of curtain materials. What to do with your settee and chairs - recover them, throw a rug over or replace them? Problems galore and you can already see the time wasted in looking around for hours trying to decide. One member of the family saying, "We want this" and another saying "Oh, no that is terrible!"

We collected a lot of junk during our time overseas. In Ireland it filled the attic, half a shed and more. When we moved, we moved it all over here, to do the same again - fill the attic, shed and more. When we finally moved to our present house, we decided it was time to do something about it. We dowsed over the lot, and are now happy to have a few choice pieces, which fit into this house. The rest was sold and we do not miss any of it.

You see, it is easy! You will find the same. Collect samples of colours and fabrics. Spread them all out, and spend a quiet half hour or so finding out which colour scheme would suit your surroundings, your furniture and your circumstances. All these questions, can be asked. Half the battle is always making up your mind, and it is very quickly done with the help of your pendulum. The result will please you, as you know it will be right. There won't be any more arguments with the others in the family.

In the end, ask where best to place your furniture, and if you have too much, ask if you should sell some of it. Will your children ever be interested in it? If not, go on a holiday on the proceeds, and enjoy the extra space in your house!!

Try a new recipe, if you don't know what to cook! Look in the fridge to see what you have, and ask which ingredients you should mix together for a delicious new dish. This could become an amazing feast, especially if you surprise your husband and friends as well. How often do Christopher and I just giggle, when I am asked how did I cook such and such a meal!

If you are a bachelor - well not only can you cook now, but what a surprise for the girl you want to impress - you cooked just what she likes to eat!! First find out what food she likes, what to drink and which flowers she likes! You can dowse over each step of cooking to ensure you are doing it the right way.

Dowse your time table and plan of action! You will become the most eligible bachelor in matters of romance.

CHAPTER 31

When metal detectors came on the market, it became a hobby for many people trying to find a treasure. How many were disappointed, when they only found old beer bottle tops or rusty nails in the garden. Yet with dowsing, you could find that 'hidden treasure' in your own garden. Make it a family occupation. Choose your questions carefully. You can ask how deep down the treasure is hidden, before you dig up the village green! However, the pendulum will not tell you how much the treasure is worth in monetary terms!!

When you are convinced that dowsing works for fun then you will believe, that it works in the same way for choosing your diet and detecting geopathic stress.

I don't want to imply that everybody is living over a geopathically stressed site. However, if you are not well, and have found that nothing really helps you, then there is a good chance that no one has yet been able to identify the cause.

If you are not confident enough to check out your own house and your own diet yourself, then before you do something drastic, let a professional dowser confirm your findings.

CHAPTER 32

"Children these days are not allowed to learn anymore", said a friend of ours, watching her daughter thoroughly enjoying herself playing in a heap of sand with our dogs. A little girl of three knew instantly how to handle our dogs, although she has none of her own and the dogs responded. Children, basically have no fear. Children and animals share a common understanding. Unless we have brought them up to fear something. When animals have been ill-treated by humans, we then can't trust them completely, as we don't know their past history, unless we know how to dowse. If we dowse, we can find out if animals can be trusted.

In Singapore we had a big garden and enough room for pets, and our boys pet rabbit had a litter. As most children who went to the same school lived in houses or apartments with little or no garden, and very few of them had pets of their own, we decided to give the other children a chance to admire our little rabbits. As soon as they had their eyes open and were big enough to be handled, we took them to the school in a small basket.

All the children were thrilled at the sight of them, except one little boy who came to me, looked at the rabbits and hardly touched one of them with one finger, and said looking very anxious "Now I will have to go and wash my hands, they (the rabbits) might have germs on them". Poor little kid. His mother or parents certainly put the fear of something into him.

Our children played in the Singapore garden all day long. There was danger from snakes, huge spiders, hornets, fire ants and big crabs. However, our boys were never in any danger during the years we were there. They were in tune with nature there, and had learnt to respect it. It was I, who panicked when I saw a big snake in the garden and insisted on killing it. Of course, accidents can happen, but the local people knew better than to kill a snake. Snakes had been in this garden long before us.

I am sure you all have watched your own or other children communicating with their pets, dogs, cats, guinea pigs, ponies. They might even have a 'secret' language with their pets. Understanding on a different level. Again, intuition on both sides.

CHAPTER 33

Christopher has a rare condition affecting his hands. After several operations his fingers became increasingly immobile and bent. His hands were not only fast closing up, but they were swollen most of the time and extremely uncomfortable. After my success of no more migraines - Christopher also went to see Mr. Thackaberry. By going through the lists of his food and materials that he was in contact with, Mr. Thackaberry found that he was, amongst other things, allergic to nylon. Nylon is used in all the labels on the back of shirts and most clothing items. "Take them out, including their stitching" Mr. Thackaberry said. "These are pressing on top of your spine against a nerve that runs to your hands, and that maybe contributing to the discomfort".

We did what Mr. Thackaberry recommended. Took out all the labels in shirts, underpants, jumpers. (My mother had an entertaining afternoon doing just that!).

Although, the mobility in Christopher's hands have not improved (it never will, as they were badly and irreversibly operated on), the pressure and the swelling went almost immediately.

I am telling this story, because how often have I heard of dowsers being called 'quacks'. Calling a dowser a quack is dismissive and you can almost hear the little box in the mind being shut, to avoid any more thought.

It is obviously much easier to be dogmatic - than to think further!

It is easier for people with unprogrammed minds - like me - to accept that dowsing works. On the other hand, a number of professional people have become dowsers and are very successful in combining their profession as doctors, engineers, scientist or army officers with their dowsing skills. Many even gave up their professions of many years to become full time dowsers.

Intuition, and that is what we as dowsers are relying on, should show the way to science as it can provide an hypothesis worth proving. The most gifted scientists are the most intuitive, however, most scientists only seem to have the five senses.

CHAPTER 34

An old sailor once said to me "A happy ship is a good ship". To me this says it all. A happy house is a good house. A happy family is a good family. If you are still sceptical maybe you don't belong to a happy crew?

We were building a house, and the whole process was a new experience for us. In the course of this, we came across one man in our team, who had a very aggressive attitude. He was an unhappy discontented person, but it was not our business to enquire why he was unhappy. He had a closed mind, so there was no point anyway.

This man had shown that he was not as good at his job as he made out, but we had no alternative, and at the time we thought, it was better to put up with the aggression than to look for somebody new, who had to be trained in.

This man went away for a few days, and almost immediately we knew, we did not want him back. It was such a relief to us when he had gone. We decided we were better off without him and would put up with the consequences.

But, what should we do? Ring up and cancel the job? At this stage, we had insufficient proof of negligence. So what could we do without offending him. The other workmen in the team would certainly hear of any trouble and the atmosphere would be spoilt.

We were told when he would be returning, but all we hoped for was that this man would not come back to work for us. The day before he was due, we heard nothing, no phone call or message. The others had not heard from him either. On the date he was supposed to start work again - again nothing, and so the time passed. Some months later he turned up for a completely different reason. He only stayed for a very short time. I managed to ask him why he had not turned up when he said he would? He answered "Nothing happened, I just did not feel like coming back".

We were astonished in one way, yet in another we had always known why he had not come back.

You might say, this is a coincidence or we treated him badly or he had another job. I appreciate that but, since then we have experienced many similar happenings.

There is a way, that we can protect ourselves and our children. You need a little bit more confidence in your dowsing ability to achieve this. Knowing what you can achieve, it would be very silly to misuse your dowsing and wish somebody bad! In our experience, It will come back to you, maybe in a round about way, but with worse results and that's not what you wanted in the first place.

"Think positively", how often have you heard or read this? But, you don't know how to go about it. Nobody told you how to do it, and it's easier said than done. Nobody is so badly off as you. You are not well, have no money, your husband is not nice, the children never listen to you, at work it's all pressure and if it wasn't for the money you wouldn't do it anyway!

If you are a gloom and doom wallower, maybe you enjoy that? Well, if you are like that, nothing will change for you, even with the best will in the world. You will always attract people who share the same gloom and doom and negativity. You and your friends don't want anything to change, because that is what you enjoy. Your problem is that you have to do something to change your circumstances, or even worse have to start to think and you don't know how!

If you were a dowser you would soon know how to change things!

First of all try to identify the negative influences around you. You have sorted out your geopathic stress? If not, maybe that is the reason you are so down? Have you improved your diet, so your body does not spend unnecessary energy in keeping going? There is a neighbour you can't stand but she keeps pestering you. You don't enjoy her company, yet you do not want to be rude. What can you do?

There is a colleague at work whose company you do not enjoy either but you can't get away from?

Sit down and relax in a safe place at home and start to sort out in your mind what in your life pulls you down. Write it down, and dowse over it with the question "Is the company of the neighbour, friend or colleague the reason you don't enjoy your work, or being at home and is this why you are miserable?"

If your life is to improve, should you stay in the job or neighbourhood or is there any other way to improve your lot? Well, as you may have guessed by now, there is another way.

Sit quietly, no TV, radio or screaming kids. If that's not possible find a quiet spot elsewhere, by a river bank, in a park or just somewhere where you can relax.

Picture your neighbour visually in your mind as you know telepathy works. Now in your relaxed state take your pendulum and let it swing freely in a "Yes" mode. You wish with all your heart that your neighbour's circumstances will improve, and that she should leave you alone. Send her all the best wishes and love you can.

With your colleague, do the same, just wish that he transfers his interest from you to somebody who would like it, and again wish him all the very best. You may not want to send your love - do the best you can! You do this, send your good wishes with your sincerest conviction and best thoughts over some time and you will be surprised what will happen.

I met a girl from South America. She is a cook in a hotel and has achieved a good position for herself. She had a friend who misused her friendship and put the girl under pressure. She was a Trainee Manager and used her authority to get the girl to cook meals for her to which she was not entitled. The situation became embarrassing, as the girl did not want to lose her job, nor did she want to inform on her so-called friend. So, one day when the whole situation became unbearable, she wished her 'friend' well, as she had always done, whenever she thought about her. Her words were "I gave it my best shot and sent her all the love I had", and she tried to cook her the best meal she had ever cooked! The situation was solved the next day. The hotel withdrew the friend's signing rights for unlimited meals.

Your children might be bullied at school and daren't say so. They cannot compete with the others in the group. They might be frightened to tell you, but, as a dowsing mother, you can check this. Protect your child from the bullies. It will not work immediately, but keep protecting your child every day. Your will is stronger and more loving, than that of the bullies. Don't wish harm to the bullies - just protect your child. They after all are only children, who are equally insecure and probably miss the love from their parents more than your children do. If you can send them good wishes - maybe nobody else does!

When you or your children need protection, you have to do this before you or your children go out, and not just a minute before. There sometimes is an awful feeling when you come back at night, that somebody might be watching you. Ask protection for when you go and, while you are out, and when you return home. It's the same as for your car but it needs a bit of dowsing confidence to achieve this.

If you have started to enjoy your dowsing even though you may not have noticed it yourself, your friends and family will certainly have noticed a change in you. Are you happier and more content with your lot? You no longer complain. You've acquired more self confidence, your attitude has changed from the negative to the positive; and you haven't even noticed! Whatever has changed in your outlook and appearance, you are obviously enjoying what you are now doing.

If you are however, a sceptic and you have managed to read this book so far and you are still not convinced, maybe some of the contents have made you think a little? Have you asked yourself why you are such a sceptic? Maybe things have always gone well for you in life, and you don't want to tempt fate. I accept that. One shouldn't anyway. As the Irish say, "Don't fix it, if it works!"

If you are however, one of these people for whom things always go wrong, perhaps you feel life is unfair. I am sure it is, but now you can examine why so much has happened to you. It's no good lamenting about it. If you try to examine it, you might not be able to pin point all the reasons, because you have to ask the right questions. Have you also thought of somebody being jealous or envious, not wishing you well? If you know where these bad wishes come from try to disperse them by wishing this person well in return. This may not make sense to you - but it will.

If you send that person good wishes with your innermost conviction, you will see that things will begin to change for you. The difficulty is, you have to be really convinced about the wishing well. If the underlying thought is not a good one, it will not work! Small changes at first, hardly noticeable, until one day you wake up and say, hey, things have improved. Well, "Thank you" tell your subconscience.

If your concern is money only - that you never have any money - maybe you have to look at your spending and find out with the help of your pendulum, in which area you can improve your financial situation. You will be given the answer.

CHAPTER 35

There are some people who meditate according to ancient rites, and feel great. They also talk about a spiritual guidance, which helps them through the day and through their lives.

With dowsing, you also will be able to put yourself into a positive frame of mind, and obtain the same spiritual elation. Think of all the good things you would like to achieve in your life. Ask your subconscience to help you with it. If you are really convinced about an important decision in your life, you can achieve it. Never mind if you can't see the way - the intuitions only come in the last possible minute. Suddenly you can see a way, which you could not have seen before.

It is very much more difficult if you wish somebody well, even if it's family, when they have a closed mind.

Yet do not give up on sending good wishes to somebody close. One day they will get there. Do it quietly, on your own, and don't tell the person concerned.

Well, you will say now with all these thoughts going backwards and forwards, why can't I try to influence the Lotto Numbers? You can try. Lotto numbers and lotteries, are random events. They cannot be predicted, but if this is all that matters to you, you must take your chance, and make your own decision.

There are days when we don't know how to get through because we have too much to do. Running here and there and everywhere and still only got half done! But it is possible to plan your day to an achievable schedule. Take a quiet ten minutes with your pendulum, and ask which way you should arrange your day to the best of your ability without stress and hassle. Make a list of all your appointments and the rest of your duties and number them. Dowse over it with the question, which is the best way to get through the day. Go through each item on your list and stick to your plan, and amazingly you'll get through! Try it - it works!

For instance, if after work you only have a short time available and you have to get to the cleaners, the chemist, the supermarket or more. Make a plan of action with your pendulum and stick to it! If you have to go to a supermarket on a Saturday, ask the day before, what time the supermarket is least crowded; and if you should go then, saving you precious time.

A girlfriend of mine had to be in hospital in the middle of London for sometime. She had a friend who visited her quite frequently. One day she arrived rather upset and hassled. She had taken a long time to find a carparking space. She said, "It was my own fault, for not asking for one ahead". My friend knew that this woman was not crazy and she was aware that this woman always seemed to know more than other people. We both now know, that this particular woman was a dowser. Before you set out to go anywhere, and you want to be able park on arrival, ask well ahead of your destination for a parking place. In my case I would say it has worked most of the times I ask. It does not work if you ask at the last minute, just before you get to your destination. The space you find may not be right outside the door where you want to go, but it will certainly will be in the close vicinity.

When your children go to school protect them from any mishaps. Before they set out, protect them every day with your love.

Sit quietly for a few minutes and think of your child or children. Take your pendulum, let it swing loosely in a "Yes" mode and start thinking that you would like to protect your children from any mishaps during the day, wherever they are.

You also can protect your husband and the ones you love and wish them well. A friend of mine told me, that she always sends love to her husband during the day. There is nothing pre-arranged between the two people. The husband will know exactly when she has sent her love to him, however busy he is.

Once you have become a dowser, you will be surprised how, out of the blue, you meet people who are on the same wave length with you. You have old friends, and you never knew that they have the same interests. All of a sudden, you meet more people with the same interest. You don't have to do very much about it, suddenly you have found a new circle of friends. When your thinking has changed, and you think much more positively about life, and how to cope with it, you attract different people around you. People whom you mistakenly thought were your friends, drop by the wayside. Do not worry; if they don't understand you that is their own choice. It's you who has changed and with a new interest in life. If you enjoy your dowsing as much as I do, it will give you such a lift in your outlook on life, that you will wonder how you have managed for so long without it.

There are programmes on TV about strange phenomena, and unexplained happenings and some history programmes. Most of these programmes leave many unanswered questions behind. Does premonition work? Does telepathy work? And many more. For dowsers, all this can be frustrating to watch. These answers can easily be obtained by dowsing.

For a retired person who has an open mind and time on their hands, what an interest this could be! To go over all the unanswered questions in history with a pendulum to find the answers! Years of work ahead and what a satisfying retirement to enjoy such a mental exercise. Dowsing is not only for the privileged or intelligent. Dowsing knows no social borders or limits. Dowsing is for everybody. If history does not interest you, you have to find a subject which does interest you! I am sure, you will find a new hobby and there must be many questions you want to know the answers to.

Premonitions. I am sure you have heard about them, but how do they work, everybody is wondering. Premonitions are dreams or flashes of very vivid pictures, usually of an imminent disaster somewhere. There have been some hoaxes, so many people fear that if they have had a premonition, they might not be taken seriously, but they should. Even if there is only

176

little time, between premonition and the actual happening, often much could be done to save people's lives. There is another thing about premonitions; we don't know when the predicted disaster will take place. These premonitions come from our subconscience and unless they are very strong in our memory we tend to brush them aside. An experienced dowser could however, check if the premonition was correct. The dowser does not have to be in the vicinity of the person who has these mental pictures. With a 'little help' a dowser can do that from a distance. Again this is not a matter for a novice dowser.

In one TV programme it was thought, that people with a simple mind could have premonitions more easily, than a sceptic. A sceptic will find it very difficult to have premonitions, as his mind is closed to anything new.

Simple people, of course find it easier to follow their sixth sense. This is the way they communicate with nature and with each other. A well known biologist went to live with the local people on an island in the Pacific. People on the island knew, when somebody had died on another island several days boat journey away! There was no communication such as telephone or radio contact. Yet they knew instantly when a person had died.

You can come to your own conclusion about that. We all have a sixth sense, as you have seen with your own children. It is just to make you aware, that we can achieve more if we encourage our children not to lose their intuitions. Keep your own intuitions alive and you might find answers nobody has thought of!

If a dowser could lead the way in research, be it medical or otherwise, valuable time could be saved to find the right answers quickly. A dowser would find it easily, especially if he knew little about the subject, and thus had no preconception of the answers.

My husband always gives me a list of fertiliser ingredients and I dowse over it to learn the needs of the land on a particular field with a particular crop. I do not know what the chemical names mean, so the left hand side of my brain cannot take over and give me the answer.

Time however, is difficult to dowse even for an experienced dowser. The subconscience does not work with a watch. If you want to dowse any questions concerning time or how quickly something can be done, don't be fooled into a quick answer. Time is something we value very much, but your intuitions do not. The answers you get may have to be treated with a pinch of salt!

However, if you decide to become a dowser with a purpose, do not forget that dowsing makes one tired. One only should dowse in an alert and happy state of mind. The same applies to the hobby dowser except he might have more time to choose from.

Agricultural research is another area with lots of rules and many sceptics. It is generally not recommended to sow clover because it is claimed that it leaches nitrates into the soil. This is a rule, and obviously according to people who make rules, this applies to every bit of land in the country. Soil is alive (anyway it should be) and has different ingredients, has been differently used or misused in the years gone by. So how can we implement such rules? Not every part of the country has the same rainfall nor the same weather conditions. If you have animals on your land, the deposits will be different from land which has no animals. By considering the conditions and present soil structure, a dowser could easily find what is missing and whether or not a crop of clover would actually improve the structure of your soil. Could we do away with the need for next years artificial fertiliser treatment. After all, clover's little stumpy roots make their own fertiliser with the help of friendly bacteria and the air.

We could discover replacement sprays for those which are too poisonous to vegetables and fruit. Maybe the chemical firms would not like such 'simple' methods of research! But they too could gain, saving funds for research programmes, to find ways and means to a healthier living for us all.

Research programmes in so many scientific fields could be geared to work together with dowsing, saving time and money. All results thereafter could easily be confirmed by scientific methods to prove their validity.

Dowsing would open up many avenues in life, give many people an interest and make our lives richer, safer and most of all happier!

CHAPTER 36

We live in a time that has opened our minds much more than in times gone past. The number of books and programmes on TV suggest that people are trying to find their own spirituality. Are religious promises still the fulfilment in everybody's life? People seem to come away more and more from religious doctrines.

Is there anything to fill the void? What about an after-life? Is there life on other planets? Do aliens exist?

With dowsing you can get an answer to all your questions. All very interesting, but I am not going to give you the answers.

I'll let you find out for yourself. So keep dowsing with an open mind!

I know that many people who have no access or no inclination to read books on a particular dowsing subject, can find a way to help themselves, the same way I have, hopefully earlier in their life than I did, but then it is never too late to pass on a good experience.

I have not gone into endless case histories in this book, this is my own story from most of my own experiences. Dowsing has saved and enlightened my life, and has helped me cross hurdles which I would not have thought possible. May it do the same for you! A sure way to happiness.

Christopher, one day, will tell you his story....

Plants that will mop-up electro-magnetic waves from your TV, computer games and other household appliances.

Botanical Name	*Common Name*
Aglaonema	Chinese Evergreen
Aloe	Aloe
Ananas	Common Pineapple
Araucaria	Norfolk Island Pine
Asplenium nidus	Bird's nest fern
Billbergia	Queen's tears
Blechnum	Brazilian tree fern
Cacti (Most) Cereus, Opuntia	Column Cactus, Bunny Ears
Calathea makoyana	Peacock plant
Calathea zebrina	Zebra plant
Cycas revoluta	Sago palm
Cyperus	Umbrella plant
Echinocactus	Barrel cactus
Ficus elastica	Rubber plant
Ficus lyrata	Fiddle leaf fig
Haworthia	Zebra haworthia, pearl plant
Phoenix	Canary date palm
Selaginella	Peacock fern, Creeping moss
Tillandsia cynea	Blue flowered torch

For further information on dowsing send a s.a.e. to

Veronika Strong
c/o DFH Publications
Shinehill Lane
South Littleton
EVESHAM
Worcs WR11 5TR

Tel: 01386 833 899
Fax: 01386 833 848
E.Mail: xia07@dial.pipex.com

Dowsing courses and consultations by appointment only.

For membership contact:
The British Society of Dowsers
Sycamore Barn,
Hastingleigh
Ashford, Kent TN25 5HW

Books recommended for further reading:-

Gifts Of Unknown Things *Lyall Watson*	The Feng Shui Handbook *Master Lam Kam Chuen*
Electro Pollution *Roger Coghill*	Earth Radiation *Kathe Bachler*
Dowsing For Health *Arthur Bailey*	Are You Sleeping in a Safe Place. *Rolf Gordon*
The Natural House Book *David Pearson*	The Celestine Prophecy The Tenth Insight *James Redfield*